INTENTIONALITY, SENSE AND THE MIND

PHAENOMENOLOGICA

COLLECTION FONDÉE PAR H.L. VAN BREDA ET PUBLIÉE
SOUS LE PATRONAGE DES CENTRES D'ARCHIVES-HUSSERL

94

MAURITA J. HARNEY

INTENTIONALITY, SENSE AND THE MIND

MAURITA J. HARNEY

INTENTIONALITY, SENSE AND THE MIND

1984 **MARTINUS NIJHOFF PUBLISHERS**
a member of the KLUWER ACADEMIC PUBLISHERS GROUP
THE HAGUE / BOSTON / LANCASTER

Distributors

for the United States and Canada: Kluwer Academic Publishers, 190 Old Derby Street, Hingham, MA 02043, USA
for the UK and Ireland: Kluwer Academic Publishers, MTP Press Limited, Falcon House, Queen Square, Lancaster LA1 1RN, England
for all other countries: Kluwer Academic Publishers Group, Distribution Center, P.O. Box 322, 3300 AH Dordrecht, The Netherlands

Library of Congress Cataloging in Publication Data

```
Harney, Maurita J.
   Intentionality, sense and the mind.

   (Phaenomenologica ; 94)
   Bibliography
   Includes index.
   1. Intention (Logic)  I. Title.  II. Series.
BC199.I5H28  1984      121'.4      83-19463
```

ISBN 90-247-2891-6 (this volume)
ISBN 90-247-2339-6 (series)

Copyright

PRINTED IN THE NETHERLANDS

FAIN WOULD I HAUE A PRETIE THING,
   TO GIUE VNTO MY LADIE:
I NAME NO THING, NOR I MEANE NO THING,
BUT AS PRETIE A THING AS MAY BEE.

> "The Lamentation of a Woman Being Wrongfully Defamed. To the tune of Damon & Pithias". *A Handefull of Pleasant Delites* by Clement Robinson and diuers others. London, 1584

ACKNOWLEDGEMENTS

The ideas in this book took shape during the 1970s at a time when Husserl scholarship was barely represented in Australian philosophical circles. I was fortunate to be working in the Philosophy Department of the Australian National University amongst colleagues who were enthusiastic in supporting my ventures into the unfamiliar terrain of European phenomenology, although their philosophical training and interests, like my own, had developed within the British analytical tradition. Of these former colleagues, I would particularly like to thank Dr. Genevieve Lloyd, Mr. Paul Thom and Dr. William Godfrey-Smith for the many hours of intensive discussion, constructive criticism and moral support which they so generously shared with me during the earlier stages of writing this work.

I extend a special thanks to Professor Max Charlesworth of Deakin University and to Professor Wolfe Mays of Manchester University for their sustained encouragement of my research over many years.

Finally, I wish to acknowledge the financial assistance which I received from the Faculty of Arts, University of Melbourne, and from the Philosophy Department of the same university towards the costs of preparing the manuscript for publication.

Melbourne, 1983   Maurita J. Harney

TABLE OF CONTENTS

INTRODUCTION

The intentionality of the mental means the object-directedness of
thought. Brentano, the acknowledged source of recent approaches
to intentionality, explains this by saying

> In presentation something is presented, in judgement something
> is affirmed or denied, in love loved, in hate hated, in desire
> desired, and so on.[1]

Reflection upon the history of the concept of intentionality since
Brentano reveals a paradox: For certain post-Wittgensteinian
philosophers of the British analytical tradition,[2] the thesis that
thought is intentional is seized upon as a way of defeating the
mentalistic consequences of Cartesian dualism, *viz.,* that thought
and its objects are private, introspectible events and items which
exist in the mind. To assert that thought is intentional is to claim
that *mental phenomena can succeed in achieving objective reference.* This is attested to by the fact that the *language* we use to
describe the object of thought in, for example, *A*'s thinking of
President Mitterrand, succeeds in referring to some existing individual and not to some private object which exists in the mind.

On the other hand, what is distinctive about the objects to
which mental phenomena are directed is that *they need not exist
in reality.* I may imagine a unicorn or think of Pegasus, even though
such objects do not exist. Brentano himself was concerned with

---

[1] Brentano (1874), p. 88.
[2] The protagonists of the "analytic" or "linguistic" versions of intentionality referred to here include Kenny, Anscombe, Geach.

the kind of existence that might be ascribed to thought-of unicorns, imagined-centaurs, and other non-existent objects of thought. This concern led him to the mentalistic conclusion that the objects to which mental phenomena are directed are "intentionally in-existent" objects – objects which are immanent to the mental act and which, therefore, exist in the mind.

The paradox then, is that, from the intentionality of the mental, some philosophers (including Brentano) have drawn mentalistic consequences, whereas other philosophers (the post-Wittgensteinians) have drawn the opposite conclusion.

Although these conclusions are incompatible, the premises from which each is derived are not inherently inconsistent with one another.

(i) The linguistic philosophers give primacy to the following:

Mental phenomena can succeed in achieving objective reference (Thesis I);

(ii) Brentano gives prominence to the following:

Mental phenomena are distinguished by the fact that their objects need not exist (Thesis II).

A satisfactory theory of intentionality must incorporate both of these theses. That is to say, our account of "objective reference" in *Thesis I* must still be consistent with *Thesis II,* so that we can preserve what is distinctive about the mental; our account of "possible non-existence" in *Thesis II* must still be consistent with *Thesis I,* so that we can avoid a mentalistic theory of objects of thought.

The central claim of this book is that *it is only by appeal to Frege's notion of sense that a satisfactory theory of intentionality can be constructed.* Chapter I provides the background to this claim by showing, first, why it is that Brentano's own theory of intentionality leads inescapably to a mentalistic theory of objects of thought, and, second, how this unwelcome consequence can be avoided if intentionality is understood as a feature of language rather than as a feature of phenomena. Chisholm's re-formulation of Brentano's intentionality thesis in terms of logical features of the sentences we use to talk about the psychological allows us to construe the question of objective reference (in *Thesis I*) as a question about *linguistic* reference rather than, as for Brentano, an ontological question about "modes of being". At the same time, the linguistic re-formulation of Brentano's thesis introduces new considerations and criteria concerning the language we use to talk about the psychological. These are the Fregean-derived criteria for the *intensionality* of language which, for Frege, are to be understood by appeal to his notion of sense.

In Chapter II we see explicitly what is involved in an appeal to Frege's notion of sense. Such an appeal commits us to accepting a three-levelled semantical framework consisting of sign, sense and referent. In terms of this framework, reference is always mediated by sense. Furthermore, it is a framework which commits us to admitting signs (i.e., names) which have a sense but which do not refer to anything. The Fregean semantical framework is contrasted with Russell's two-levelled semantical framework consisting only of sign (i.e., name) and referent. In terms of the Russellian framework reference is unmediated by sense; names necessarily refer to some existing thing. (There can be no signs i.e., names, which lack a reference). If we invoke the Fregean three-levelled semantical framework to explicate intentionality, then "objective reference" in *Thesis I* is to be understood as that which is mediated by sense; because within the Fregean framework we can admit signs which have a sense but which do not refer to anything, we can also allow for "possible non-existence of objects of thought" in *Thesis II*. Frege provides us with the appropriate semantical framework for saying *both* that mental phenomena can succeed in achieving objective reference (*Thesis I*) *and* that they may fail to do so (*Thesis II*). But, in both cases, it is the notion of sense which is crucial.

Problems arise for a theory of intentionality if we accept the Russellian two-levelled framework in place of the Fregean one in explicating objective reference in *Thesis I*. These problems are discussed in Chapter III in connection with the relational theory of thoughts about existing objects. This theory derives from Russell's theory of names. The logical consequence of this approach to objective reference in *Thesis I* is the reduction of the mental to the physical and, ultimately, the repudiation of the intentional altogether.

Problems of a different kind arise for the "irreducibility theorists" when Fregean sense is (either explicitly or implicitly) ignored. These theorists endorse Chisholm's claim (derived from

Brentano) that intentionality is irreducible — sentences about the mental cannot be translated into sentences about the physical. The problems for the irreducibility theorist arise from the attempt to say *both* that intentionality is distinctive of all and only mental phenomena *and* that the object of a mental act can be "objective" in precisely the same way that the object of a physical act is "objective". The difficulties for the irreducibility theorist are exemplified in Anscombe's attempts to provide an account of the intentionality of perception. These are discussed in Chapter IV. This discussion serves to make explicit some of the presuppositions involved in Anscombe's setting up of the problems of intentionality. Unlike the relational theorists, there is nothing which is explicitly *anti*-Fregean in Anscombe's account. But neither can we say that there is anything specifically Fregean about the framework within which Anscombe approaches the problem of intentionality. In a later discussion — Chapter VI — it emerges that Anscombe's framework is fundamentally incompatible with a Fregean semantical framework which admits the notion of sense.

The characterisation of "objective reference" in *Thesis I* in terms of a two-levelled semantical framework (whether this be an explicit acceptance of a Russellian theory of reference, or an implicit neglect of Frege's notion of sense) is one successful way of avoiding a mentalistic theory of objects of thought. But this success is at the expense of either (a) relinquishing the intentionality of those acts, or (b) creating intractable problems for an attempt to state that acts which *are* intentional *can* succeed in achieving objective reference.

These problems are avoided if we appeal to Frege's notion of sense in affirming *Theses I* and *II*. To make this claim, however, we must be able to meet an objection raised by certain post-Fregean philosophers of language — *viz.*, that the notion of sense is tied to a mentalistic theory of meaning. Quine, for example, argues that senses or intensions (i.e., meanings) are entities which exist in the mind. A more serious objection is raised by Putnam who argues that, because senses or intensions are "mind-related" (i.e., what is grasped in an act of understanding the meaning of a term), meaning *qua* sense has merely psychological status. If Putnam's argument is justified, then the Fregean thesis that reference is determined by sense must be seen as a "psychologistic" theory of the determination of reference: one which holds that reference is determined by "merely psychological" considerations. Our task in Chapter V will be to specify precisely what kind of "mentalistic" theory is ascribed to Frege by these critics. Here we will see that in order to meet the charge of mentalism we must, on Frege's behalf, be able to offer an account of how sense (i.e., meaning) relates to the mind without thereby introducing a psychologistic theory of meaning and reference.

Frege himself does not provide us with such a theory, although as a committed adversary of psychologism, he would certainly have resisted these criticisms. In order to counter the accusation of mentalism, therefore, *it is necessary to supplement Frege's theory of sense with a non-psychologistic theory of the way in which sense or meaning can be at once "mind-related" and a means to objective reference.* In Chapter VI it will be argued that this supplementation is to be provided by a phenomenological account of linguistic meaning and reference which is based on Husserl's theory of the intentionality of acts of consciousness. Husserl's theory of linguistic meaning and reference is initially proposed as part of a deliberate attack on psychologistic theories of meaning. In Husserl's theory, a psychological approach to meaning is replaced by a phenomenological one. The semantical framework for his theory of meaning and reference is the Fregean three-levelled one, in which reference is mediated by meaning, and in which signs (names) which have a meaning but which do not refer to anything are admitted. For Husserl, however, the semantical framework of name, meaning, referent is one which results from a theory of the intentionality of acts of consciousness — a theory which tells us that, to every act, there corresponds a meaning through which some object is intended. In terms of this kind of theory, the "mind-relatedness" of linguistic meaning or sense is to be explained by saying that the latter is an intentional notion — one tied to the intentionality of acts. At the same time, the meaning (or "noema") of an intentional act is the *means by which* we intend something objective. A theory of intentionality which invokes Husserl's notion of the "noema" provides us with a non-psychologistic account of the way in which Fregean sense can be both mind-related and a "vehicle for objective reference".[3]

[3] Olafson (1975), p. 76: "Intentionality is . . . the basic vehicle of objective reference generally and thus of our knowledge of the world which Husserl speaks of as a comprehensive intentional object".

In the development of the main argument of this book, two important philosophical traditions are brought together: On the one hand, we have the British analytical tradition, represented here by Chisholm, Anscombe, Russell and the post-Russellian philosophers of language, Quine, Putman and Kripke; on the other hand, we have the phenomenological tradition represented by its founder, Husserl. In the context of the present work, each of these traditions provides a background to two different lines of approach to the topic of intentionality. Philosophers of the analytical tradition approach this topic by way of an investigation of logic and language, whereas those who follow the tradition of Husserl's phenomenology approach this same topic by way of an investigation of the acts and structures of human consciousness. In bringing these two traditions together, it has been my aim to show how each might inform, and be informed by, the other.

The groundwork for such a project, where intentionality is concerned, has already been laid by those writers who have sought to extend the insights of Brentano, on the one hand, and of Frege, on the other, beyond the bounds of the tradition with which each is commonly associated. Brentano was one of the most important influences on the shaping of Husserl's phenomenological philosophy and is justifiably numbered amongst the significant precursors of that tradition. However, it was Brentano who provided the main inspiration behind Chisholm's attempt to develop a "linguistic" approach to intentionality — an attempt which, in turn, generated extensive debate within analytical circles concerning the relation between intentionality and intensionality. In the case of Frege, there can be no question of the latter's significance in laying the foundations of the analytical movement which has dominated British and Northern American philosophy in recent years. But recent researches, initiated by Føllesdal's important thesis which drew explicit parallels between the ideas of Frege and of Husserl,[4] have succeeded in showing us how a study of Frege's philosophy might contribute to an understanding of Husserl's thought. The approach to intentionality which is undertaken in this book owes much to the work of writers like Chisholm and Føllesdal who, in

[4] Føllesdal (1969).

very different ways, have commenced the task of bridging the gap in understanding between the two traditions.[5]

Attempts to align key figures and ideas across very different traditions inevitably invite controversy. The connections urged in this book are no exception: Chisholm's attempts to incorporate Brentano's insights into an analytical framework stimulated lively and persistent debate at the time, and, more recently, the relation between Chisholm's own theory and that of Brentano has come under critical scrutiny.[6] The connection between the ideas of Husserl and of Frege, first explicitly spelled out by Føllesdal, has also been the subject of much discussion in recent years. Debates such as these play an important part in showing us the extent and the limits to which connections across differing traditions can be drawn. This book seeks to extend and develop many of these debates by showing how the relevant relationships might be illuminated and strengthened within the limits set by differing backgrounds and traditions of those ideas and thinkers.

Relationships commonly assumed to obtain within a single tradition must also be subject to scrutiny, however. The arguments in this book invite a re-appraisal of the Frege-Russell alliance which is uncritically presupposed by some writers of the analytical tradition. Such re-appraisal does not amount to a denial of Frege's influence on Russell or of their shared aims in constructing logical systems applicable to the analysis of language. Rather, what is called for here is recognition of the limits to which this alliance can be urged. I have argued here that Frege's notion of sense lies beyond these limits — that, in respect of the notion of sense, Frege must be distanced from Russell. The semantical framework for the theory of intentionality attempted in this book is fundamentally incompatible with that of Russell, and the notion of sense to which that theory appeals has no counterpart in Russell's theory of language. It is only by driving this wedge between Frege and Russell in respect of this notion that we can defend Frege against the charge of psychologism and admit the possibility of drawing the required parallels with Husserl's philosophy.

[5] Significant contributions to this task have appeared since the completion of the present work. These include Mohanty (1982), Smith and McIntyre (1982), and Dreyfus (ed.), (1982).

[6] Howarth (1980).

Similarly, within the corpus of Husserl's writings about the relation between meaning and the mind, it is necessary to deviate from a more orthodox or literal thematic approach which might seek to locate Husserl's theory of sense and reference solely within his *Logical Investigations* of 1900–1901. It is in this work that we find an explicit formulation of a theory of the relationship between intentional acts and the sense and reference of expressions. However, the Husserlian theory of linguistic meaning that is urged in the present work is one which follows logically from Husserl's *later* work, *Ideas I* (1913) – the work in which his theory of meaning-as-noema is developed, albeit in relation to perception. *Ideas I* carries the recommendation that linguistic sense and reference be understood by appeal to the noema of intentional acts, but there is no explicit formulation of a semantic theory, here. The phenomenological approach to linguistic sense and reference which is introduced in the concluding chapter for purposes of supplementing Frege's theory is one which requires that we reverse the chronology of the development of Husserl's theory of meaning and, as it were, undertake a reading of certain aspects of the *Logical Investigations* through the conceptual and methodological framework of the later *Ideas I*.

The eclecticism of drawing connections between ideas *across* different traditions, like that of creating new connections within a single tradition or within the writings of a single author, is not without its dangers. The ideas of the key figures discussed in this book – Brentano, Frege and Husserl – have emerged from vastly different contexts and concerns. To ignore these underlying differences is to risk distorting the comparisons and contrasts that can be drawn at the theoretical level.

Brentano's main concern was with the subject-matter of psychology. He sought to discover some identifying feature of mental phenomena – some feature which characterised all mental phenomena and which would succeed in distinguishing the latter from the phenomena studied by the physical sciences. For Brentano, intentionality was said to be the feature which served this purpose.

By contrast, Frege's interests lay in the direction of mathematics and of logic, his innovatory work in these areas providing the foundations of modern philosophical and mathematical logic. Frege's aim was to set mathematics on a rigorous logical basis and to this end he waged an unremitting campaign against psychologistic theories of the meaning of mathematical concepts — theories which confused the meaning of these concepts with the private contents of individual mental acts or processes. Frege's celebrated distinction of "sense" (*Sinn*) and "reference" (*Bedeutung*) was crucial to his attack on psychologistic theories of linguistic meaning in general.

The aims of Husserl's *Logical Investigations* bear a *prima facie* similarity to those of Frege. We see in this work Husserl's commitment to anti-psychologism and his professed aim of establishing logic on a rigorous scientific basis. But whereas for Frege this task was seen as a *logical* one — i.e., the construction of logical systems — for Husserl the perceived task was an *epistemological* one. The ideal of rigour was, for Husserl, synonymous with the ideal of bringing epistemological clarity and justification to the laws and concepts of logic. He believed that the way to achieving this ideal was through an investigation of the origins of our knowledge of these laws and concepts in subjective acts of consciousness. Husserl rightly perceived that empirical psychology was inadequate to perform this task for it would fail to account for the necessity pertaining to these laws and concepts, and would lead instead to psychologistic consequences. Instead, he advocated a phenomenological approach to this kind of investigation. His phenomenological method, introduced in the first instance to secure a sound epistemological foundation for logic, was subsequently developed by Husserl as a methodology for investigating acts of consciousness, generally. It was in the context of this subsequent development — specifically in relation to perception in *Ideas I* — that Husserl's noematic approach to meaning assumed a significant role. For it was this approach which opened up the possibility of a new kind of investigation — an investigation not into acts themselves but into the objective *correlates* of those acts: their noematic structures.

It is from this diverse array of aims and preoccupations that certain key ideas in this book have been drawn. These ideas, I believe, can make a positive contribution to our understanding of intentionality and to the unravelling of certain problems that surround that topic. This book is an attempt to demonstrate the nature and importance of that contribution whilst at the same time paying due respect to the differences where the authorship of those ideas is concerned.

CHAPTER I

INTENTIONALITY, MENTALISM, AND THE PROBLEM OF OBJECTIVE REFERENCE

§ 1. *Introduction: intentionality and the denial of mentalism*

One consequence of Wittgenstein's celebrated arguments against the possibility of a private language has been the release of "the mental" from "mentalism". Quinton writes:

The particular philosophical problem that takes up most of Wittgenstein's attention in the *Investigations* is that of the nature of mind or, in his terminology, of the language in which we report and describe the mental states of ourselves and others. The metaphysical doctrine against which he is arguing here is that persistent dualism of mind and body, made explicit by Plato and Descartes, but, it would seem, rather deeply lodged in our ordinary way of thinking, which holds that mental states exist in private worlds of their own of which only one person is directly aware. The paradoxes arising from this theory are, first and foremost, the idea that we can never know what is going on in the mind of another person and also perhaps the older difficulty about understanding how things can act upon each other when they are as different from one another as mental and bodily states are according to this theory. The mistaken analogy that lies behind the skeptical absurdities of dualism is that between "I see a tree" or "I touch this stone" on the one hand and "I feel a pain" and "I understand this calculation" on the other. Just as the first two sentences report perception of and action on physical things, so, it is supposed, the other two report mental perception and action. The world is then conceived as containing, alongside material objects and acts of manipulating them, mental objects like pains and mental acts or processes like understanding, meaning and thinking.[1]

Metaphysical dualism is objectionable because it implies the view that our mental vocabulary acquires its meaning from introspection upon essentially inner or private states and processes. Mental words, such as "pain" are names of private objects. Against this view, Wittgenstein argues that our mental vocabulary acquires its meaning from the public and shareable language to which it belongs. If mental words acquire their meaning as the result of a private ostensive definition, then there is no way of explaining how the meanings of those words could be communicated. The criteria for the application of mental words must be publicly observable events and dispositions. Therefore the meaning of mental words cannot be some private object referred to or named by that word. Wittgenstein's own arguments against the notion of a private object are concerned primarily with a sensation, *viz.*, pain. But, as Kenny points out,

> With the emotions, the Cartesian idea of a purely mental event runs into an extra difficulty. Emotions, unlike pain, have objects: we are afraid *of* things, angry *with* people, ashamed *that* we have done such-and-such. This feature of the emotions, which is sometimes called their 'intentionality',[2] is misrepresented by Descartes, who treats the relation between a passion and its object as a contingent one of effect to cause.[3]

The principle that Kenny is alluding to here is the intentionality of the mental. To say that mental phenomena are intentional is to say that they are directed to some object: All thinking is thought *of* something, all fearing is fear *of* something, all hoping is hope *for* something, and so forth. The relation between thought and its object is a logical relation in the sense that there cannot *be* a

---

[1] Quinton (1964), p. 17.

[2] Kenny's original spelling of this word is "intensionality". For reasons which will emerge later, I have adopted the spelling "intentionality".

[3] Kenny (1963), pp. 13–14.

thinking, hoping, fearing, etc., without there being *something* which is thought, hoped for, feared, etc.

"Objects" of thought are, for the most part, things which exist independently of the thinking, or – in the case of cognitive activities such as understanding, believing, knowing – propositions which are true or false independently of the act of understanding, knowing, etc. By attending to the language that we use to describe such "objects", we can see that they are not to be regarded as private mental items belonging to the realm of the mental: If I think of President Mitterrand or if I admire Simone de Beauvoir, the words giving the "object" of my thought succeed in referring to the real existing individual in each case, and not to some private item or mental image of that individual. Similarly, if I understand Pythagoras' theorem or believe that $2 + 2 = 4$, then *what* I grasp in understanding or *what* I believe – *viz.*, some proposition – is something that is public and shareable in the sense that it may be grasped or believed by others. It is for this reason that such propositions are amenable to judgements of truth or falsity. In short, *mental phenomena* – acts of thinking, fearing, understanding, etc., – *can succeed in achieving "objective reference"*. (*Thesis I*).

If mental phenomena are conceived of in dualistic terms – that is, in terms of the metaphysical dualism of mind and body outlined by Quinton – then we cannot maintain the claim that mental phenomena can succeed in achieving objective reference. For if the relation between thought and its object is a logical relation (i.e., not merely a contingent relation of effect to cause), then both thought *and* its object will belong to the realm of the mental: If thinking – the mental act – is confined to the domain of the non-physical, then the object to which that act is logically related will also be confined to that domain. This is a "mentalistic" view of objects of thought.

The words "mentalistic" and "mentalism" are used to describe any theory which holds, or which implies as a consequence, the view that "objects of thought" have merely mental existence or merely psychological status.[4] On such a view, the status – existential

---

[4] Although the words "mentalism" and "psychologism" occur frequently in philosophical literature, it is rare to find any precise specification of what these terms mean. In keeping with this practice, my initial characterisation of these terms is deliberately left general.

or otherwise — of objects of thought depends upon the mental act to which it is related. Thus, *things* which are thought of, perceived, wanted, etc., are said to be entities which exist in the mind. This kind of mentalism I shall call "ontological mentalism". Alternatively, one may hold that the objects of cognitive acts such as the laws of logic or of mathematics have merely psychological status, in the sense that inquiries into these laws and their associated concepts are, at a fundamental level, psychological inquiries — inquiries about mental processes or activities. This form of mentalism is generally known as "psychologism". In subsequent chapters, it will be necessary to refine and to specify more closely these varieties of mentalism. But the general point to be observed here is that mentalistic theories deny *Thesis I* — they do not allow for the possibility that mental phenomena can succeed in achieving objective reference.

In summary, by appeal to linguistic considerations — specifically the language we use to talk about mental phenomena — we are able to assert that mental phenomena can succeed in achieving objective reference. This is to be understood as the claim that objects of thought need not be private mental items or have merely psychological status. To assert that mental phenomena can succeed in achieving objective reference is, therefore, to avoid a mentalistic theory of objects of thought.

But what is the price we pay for accepting *Thesis I*, that mental phenomena can succeed in achieving objective reference? Do we thereby lose what is distinctive about the mental — *viz., that mental phenomena are distinguished by the fact that the objects to which they are directed need not exist (Thesis II)*? For some philosophers, the thesis that mental phenomena can succeed in achieving objective reference is taken to imply that there is nothing distinctive about the mental — "mentalism" is avoided by dispensing with "the mental" and, therewith, intentionality. Our explication of the notion of "objective reference" in *Thesis I* will, therefore, be of crucial importance where any attempts to combine *Theses I* and *II* are concerned. However before we can proceed to an examination of this notion, we must first consider the second thesis required for a theory of intentionality — its origins in, and its implications for Brentano's thought, and its reformulation in terms of linguistic criteria.

§2. Brentano's thesis of intentionality

Brentano states his thesis of intentionality as follows:

> Every mental phenomenon is characterised by what the Scholastics of the Middle Ages called the intentional (or mental) in-existence of an object, and what we might call, though not wholly unambiguously, reference to a content, direction upon an object (which is not to be understood here as meaning a thing), or immanent objectivity. Every mental phenomenon includes something as an object within itself, although they do not all do so in the same way. In presentation something is presented, in judgment something is affirmed or denied, in love loved, in hate hated, in desire desired, and so on.
>
> This intentional in-existence is characteristic exclusively of mental phenomena. No physical phenomenon exhibits anything like it. We can, therefore, define mental phenomena by saying that they are those phenomena which contain an object intentionally within themselves.[5]

Brentano's intentionality thesis states that, for any mental activity, there is always some object to which that activity is directed. I cannot think without thinking something, I cannot hope without hoping for something. But the peculiarity of the objects of mental activities is that they need not exist. No physical phenomena exhibit this characteristic. If I kick a stone or eat an apple, there must exist some stone that I kick or some apple that I eat. But if I think of a stone or wish for an apple, it does not follow from this that such objects exist.

What Brentano means by "mental phenomena" and "physical phenomena", then, is to be understood in terms of dichotomy of *act* and *object. Possible non-existence of the object of a mental act is what distinguishes mental from physical phenomena (Thesis II).* Brentano, then, provides us with the second of the theses required for a theory of intentionality. However, when we examine Brentano's own elaboration of this thesis, we find that it leads to the mentalistic conclusion that objects of thought are immanent to the act of thinking: they are objects which exist in the mind.

[5] Brentano (1874), pp. 88–9.

Chisholm[6] points out that Brentano's doctrine of intentionality contains both an ontological thesis and a psychological thesis: The ontological thesis concerns the "intentional in-existence" of objects of thought; the psychological thesis tells us that thought is always directed. Like Chisholm, I shall deal with each of these in turn although the direction and emphases of my discussion will be significantly different from those of Chisholm's.

For Brentano the "problem of intentionality" concerned the possible non-existence of objects of thought. His primary concern was with non-existing objects of thought — thought-of centaurs, imagined unicorns, etc. He saw the problem of the possible non-existence of objects of thought as an ontological problem concerning the existential status of these non-existing objects of thought. For Brentano, the question to be raised of such objects is: What kind of being do they have? There is a difference between a man who is thinking of a horse and a man who is thinking about a unicorn. But this difference cannot consist in the fact that the first man's thinking has an object where the second man's does not. For this would be a difference between a man who is thinking and a man who is not thinking.[7] If a man is thinking about a unicorn then the object of his thought is a unicorn. But it cannot be a real existing unicorn. Therefore the thought-of unicorn must have a mode of being other than real existence. In this way the problem concerning objects of thought is seen, by Brentano, to be an ontological problem concerning the existential status of objects of thought.

There seem to be two possible ways of answering the question,

---

[6] Chisholm (1967), p. 6.

[7] cf. Plato's Theaetetus, 189a—b:

Soc. And does not he who thinks, think some one thing?
Theaet. Certainly.
Soc. And does not he who thinks some one thing, think something which is?
Theaet. I agree.
Soc. Then he who thinks of that which is not, thinks of nothing?
Theaet. Clearly.
Soc. And he who thinks of nothing, does not think at all?
Theaet. Obviously.
Soc. Then no one can think that which is not, either as a self-existent substance or as a predicate of something else?
Theaet. Clearly not.

What kind of being can be ascribed to objects of thought which do not have real existence? One possibility is to say of such objects that they have a mode of being like that of Meinong's winged horse or Golden Mountain which are accorded the status of *ausserseiend* ("beyond being"). If this were the case, then, when X is thinking of a unicorn, we would say of X that he is intentionally related to an "extra-mental non-entity, that is, something that, strictly speaking, does not *exist* (i.e., is *ausserseiend*) but still has an independent ontological status".[8] Alternatively, one could ascribe to such objects some kind of existence-in-the-mind. This is the view which Brentano in fact subscribed to. When X is thinking of a unicorn, there is produced an intentionally in-existent object which is an entity in addition to the individual thinker.[9] Thus the object to which X is intentionally related is an intra-mental entity. On this view the word "intentional" applies to an intra-mental act and an intra-mental object, in which case the "doctrine of intentionality is indefeasibly and objectionably 'mentalistic'".[10]

One major difficulty with attempting to ascribe ontological status to non-existing objects of thought is that such attempts often involve the violation of the law of non-contradiction. One can think about something that is contradictory. If the object of my thought enjoys some peculiar mode of being, then we can ascribe to that "object" the contradictory properties of being both A and not-A.[11]

There are difficulties *both* with the Meinongian view which ascribes the extra-mental status of *ausserseiend* to objects of thought, *and* with the mentalistic view which relegates to such

[8] Carr (1975), p. 33.
[9] Chisholm (1967) points out that, in Brentano's later writings of 1914, the notion of an intentionally in-existent object as something which exists *in addition to* the person thinking is abandoned in favour of the "reistic" view according to which saying that there *is* an immanent object is to say no more than that there *is* an actual person who is thinking about that object.
[10] Olafson (1975), p. 75.
[11] *cf.* Russell (1904). Furthermore, Chisholm (1967) points out that almost all intentionally in-existent objects violate the law of excluded middle. I may promise you an ox and presumably it has a head, tail, etc., and is heavy. But, Chisholm asks, is it such that it weighs 817 pounds, or is it such that it does not weigh 817 pounds? We must answer both of these questions in the negative.

objects a form of existence in the mind. Both of these views fail to account for the situation in which X is thinking of something which does exist. If, for example, I am thinking of the Eiffel Tower then it is the real existing object to which I am intentionally related. It is not some entity – either extra-mental *or* intra-mental – which exists *in addition to* the real thing. Even in cases where the object is not known for certain, as in Diogenes' looking for an honest man, then it is a real concrete individual that he is looking for and not some intentionally in-existent object (which, if it exists in Diogenes' mind has already been found).[12]

These difficulties arise as a result of considerations concerning thoughts that are directed to "external non-mental" objects, and Brentano's own understanding of these objects was based on a fundamentally dualistic ontology. Olafson points out:

> The external non-mental object in fact plays no part at all in Brentano's account of the intentional object, because he understands the former in basically dualistic representationalist terms . . . In other words, in his work the adjective "intentional" applies exclusively to an intra-mental object and to an equally intra-mental act in its relationship to that object while the broader question of the mind-world relationship is handled by Brentano in perfectly conventional realist and dualist terms.[13]

Here Olafson is implicitly acknowledging Chisholm's separation of Brentano's ontological thesis from his psychological thesis concerning intentionality. Olafson is saying, in effect, that Brentano's ontological thesis, within which questions concerning the existential status of objects of thought can be raised, is set against a straightforwardly dualistic framework. However for Olafson, the word "intentional" describes those objects which, on the psychological thesis, are said to be correlated with acts. This explication is not, of course, presented as a defence of Brentano against the charge of mentalism – Brentano's doctrine remains "indefeasibly and objectionably mentalistic". But, it does suggest that Brentano's mentalism is a consequence of the juxtaposition of an ontological

---

[12] *cf*. Chisholm (1967), p. 11.
[13] Olafson (1975), p. 75.

thesis with his psychological thesis and, moreover, it invites us to consider the intentionality thesis in the setting of this psychological thesis in isolation from the ontological concerns.

The main features of this setting of the psychological thesis are Brentano's descriptive psychology and his theory of presentations based on the dichotomy of act and object.

For Brentano, intentionality is the most important characteristic which distinguishes mental from physical phenomena. Brentano's aim in drawing this distinction is to circumscribe and specify the subject-matter of the "science of the mental". Mental phenomena which constitute this domain must be distinguished from physical phenomena which constitute the subject-matter of the "science of the physical". Specifically for Brentano the "science of the mental" is his descriptive psychology. Descriptive psychology is the description of mental phenomena or activities from the point of view of the experiencing subject. We might characterise it in a loose preliminary way as "psychology from a 'first-person' perspective". Descriptive psychology is not the same as empirical psychology (what Brentano calls "genetic" or "explanatory" psychology). The concern of empirical psychology is the processes and causal connections, including physiological ones, whereby we theorise about or explain the workings of the mind. Empirical psychology proceeds from a standpoint outside that of the first-person perspective. Brentano's criteria for the mental must, therefore, be compatible with the perspective of his descriptive psychology -- his class of mental phenomena must be *descriptively* marked.

Strict adherence to the descriptive method precludes any appeal to "transcendent realities" in our characterisation of the mental. If our concern is solely the description of the modes in which phenomena are presented to consciousness, then, strictly speaking, metaphysical distinctions and theories will play no part in this enterprise. This helps to make sense of Olafson's remark that "the external non-mental object . . . plays no part in Brentano's account of the intentional object . . . ".[14] For, in terms of Brentano's psychological thesis alone, the word "intentional" belongs to the description of what appears to consciousness.

[14] *Ibid.*

By isolating Brentano's psychological thesis in this way we can show a significant difference between Brentano's and Descartes' characterisations of "the mental". Both philosophers wished to distinguish the class of the mental from the class of physical phenomena. But Brentano's distinction is motivated by his concern to develop a descriptive psychology; Descartes' aim, on the other hand, was to discover the ultimate certainties on which all knowledge is founded, and the epistemological distinction between privately-accessible certain knowledge, on the one hand, and observationally-based public knowledge, on the other, are taken to be marks of two separate realms of possible knowledge — the domains of the mental and the physical. Brentano, who was in fact a great admirer of Descartes, makes use of Descartes' notion of the "self-evidently given" as a feature of the mental. However for Brentano, self-evidence is a *descriptive* feature of the mode in which mental phenomena are given rather than, as for Descartes, an *epistemological* feature of a metaphysical category, *viz.*, the realm of the mental. The concern of Brentano's descriptive psychology is the description of phenomena as "appearances to consciousness", where self-evidence is a feature of such appearances. In short, Descartes' "mental phenomena" are characterised relative to a theory of what is *real* — a metaphysical theory; Brentano's "mental phenomena" are characterised relative to a description of the mode in which phenomena are given — a descriptive psychology.

Brentano states that all mental phenomena are presentations or are based on presentations. By "presentation" he means "not that which is presented but the act of presentation."[15] Brentano gives as examples, "hearing a sound, seeing a coloured object, feeling warmth or cold, . . .".[16] Cognitive acts such as thinking as a concept, judging, recollecting, as well as emotions — joy, sorrow, fear, etc., — are based on presentations and are therefore included within the class of mental phenomena. Brentano explains what he means by "an *act* of presentation" by drawing attention to an ambiguity in the word "pain".[17] This word can be used to describe

[15] Brentano (1874), p. 85.
[16] *Ibid.*, p. 79.
[17] *Ibid.*, p. 84.

the physical phenomenon – the physical cut or burn – or it can refer to the feeling which accompanies the physical injury. It is the latter "act"[18] of feeling or sensing pain, and not the external physical stimulation, which is the presentation.

Presentations exist whenever something appears in consciousness, "whether it be hated or loved or regarded indifferently. . . . As we use the word 'to present', 'to be presented' comes to mean the same thing as 'to appear'."[19] Feelings and sensations are not to be regarded as external or bodily stimulations which are followed by presentations. Rather, in the very sensing of the change in one's state, presentations are involved. As soon as such stimulations are designated as feelings or sensations, there is already implicit reference to a presentation.[20]

In summary, Brentano takes "presentation" to mean
(i) the act of presenting (in contrast to that which is presented);
(ii) the appearance to consciousness (in contrast to external or physical phenomena with which such appearances are associated).

Brentano's remarks concerning "inner perception" serve to illuminate what he means by "mental phenomena" – the subject-matter of his psychology – as well as his notion of a presentation. Mental phenomena alone are the objects of inner perception; physical phenomena are the objects of outer perception. Inner perception is said to be immediate, self-evident and infallible. If mental phenomena constitute the domain of descriptive psychology, then

---

[18] Brentano sometimes uses the words "mental activity" interchangeably with "mental phenomenon". The words "act" and "activity", here, are not to be confused with "activity" in the sense of process. It does seem that these words pertain to the "act-uality" which characterises mental phenomena as immediately given. In an editor's note to Brentano's work (*Ibid.*, p. 79 note 1), it is pointed out that the word "activity" means "being concerned with something" or "having something as object". This means that Brentano's notion of "act" or "activity" must be contrastable with "passivity" in the sense which implies that mental phenomena involve the passive reception of sense data. If mental phenomena were not considered to be activities in *this* sense, then their investigation would be a matter of tracing causal connections, responses to stimuli, etc., all of which, for Brentano, are excluded from the domain of his descriptive psychology.

[19] *Ibid.*, p. 81.
[20] *Ibid.*, pp. 82–3.

Brentano's concern is solely with what is immediately and self-evidently given in perception. He says: "Strictly speaking, so-called external perception is not perception. Mental phenomena, therefore, may be described as the only phenomena of which perception in the strict sense of the word is possible".[21] By this, it seems, Brentano means that "outer perception" belongs to the domain of the physical sciences, and an investigation of the phenomena of outer perception will be an investigation into physiological processes, causal connections, etc. Perception *qua* psychological act – i.e., the *experience* of perceiving – involves a presentation, and must therefore be described *as* a presentation, in which case it is what appears to consciousness which is to be described. Perception, in this sense, is not to be understood in terms of a relation between the perceiver and some external or non-mental object, but rather in terms of a relation to an object which is *immanent* to that act.

This means, of course, that questions concerning veridical as opposed to non-veridical "perception" do not fall within the subject-matter of a descriptive psychology such as Brentano's. This re-inforces the point made earlier, that Brentano is not concerned to offer a theory of what is "real" (in the metaphysical sense[22]) nor a theory of how or whether we can know "the real". The "objects of thought" in the case of presentations must be taken to mean objects *immanent to* the act of presenting.

It is against this background of a theory of presentations belonging to descriptive psychology that Brentano's intentionality thesis is set. "Intentionality" – directedness to an object – is what characterises mental phenomena – i.e. presentations. Presentations, then, must be understood in terms of the dichotomy of act and object. But, clearly, this way of characterising mental phenomena falls short of giving us a mark which *distinguishes* mental from physical phenomena. It is in response to the need for a distinguishing

[21] *Ibid.*, p. 19.

[22] For Brentano, it is descriptive psychology which is distinguished by the fact that it is concerned with "phenomena which are *known immediately as true and real in themselves*". (*Ibid.*, p. 20n.) Here, Brentano is not ascribing *metaphysical* reality to mental phenomena, for if he were, his theory would be an idealist one and, therefore, susceptible to the charge of self-contradictoriness. The "real" (or actual) is the self-evidently given for Brentano.

feature of mental phenomena that Brentano ascribes "intentional in-existence" to the objects of mental acts thereby introducing the ontological thesis with its implied dualism.

The introduction of the ontological thesis, here, constitutes a departure from a purely descriptive account of mental acts and their objects. A purely descriptive method allows us to distinguish act and object in the case of a presentation, but, strictly speaking, the object of the act is *ontologically* neutral, in terms of this approach. This suggests that we might release Brentano's psychological thesis from the ontological one,[23] and thereby avoid the problems inherent in talking about modes of *existence* of objects of thought. Presentations are "appearances to consciousness". One way of signalling the removal of the ontological thesis with its questions about the existential status of *what it is* that is given to consciousness, is to interpret Brentano's dichotomy of act and object, in the case of presentations, as a distinction between the act and the *content* of a presentation. This means that a description of "objects of thought" is to consist in a description of what is given or contained in a particular experience, regardless of what, if anything, that experience is an experience *of*.

However, to isolate Brentano's psychological thesis in this way is not to escape mentalism. It means, rather, than any attempt to provide a theory of "objects of thought" based on this thesis will ultimately be vulnerable to the charge of *psychologism*. For, on Brentano's theory of presentations, the "object" (i.e. the content) is that which is immanent to the act — it is, literally, something which is "contained in" the particular act of presentation. This means that inquiries into "objects of thought" will ultimately be psychological inquiries into subjective psychological acts or experiences.

"Psychologism" is a word that is generally applied to certain theories about the *cognitive* objects of thought — propositions which are grasped, understood, asserted, judged, etc. Such "objects" include necessary truths such as the laws of mathematics and of logic. These laws are said to have *logical* status in that they

---

[23] This recommendation is implicit in Olafson (1975), and it is explicit in Chisholm (1967) who argues that, by shedding Brentano's ontological thesis, we can then understand his doctrine of intentionality as stating simply the "having of something in mind".

are necessarily true, independently of whether anyone believes them to be so. A psychologistic theory of such laws is one which, either explicitly or implicitly, ascribes to such laws merely psychological status by making them part of the data of a psychological inquiry.

We can distinguish two kinds of psychologism in respect of such "objects".[24] First, there is "reductive" psychologism such as Hume's. According to this form of psychologism, the truths of logic and mathematics are reduced to empirical generalisations about mental processes: the necessity of such truths is reduced to the universality of certain thought processes. On this particular view, there is no difficulty in asserting that such truths are publicly knowable. The fact that we express these truths as generalisations means that the thought processes are shared.

The second form of psychologism — that which results from Brentano's theory of presentations — is what we might call "subjective" psychologism. Here, the separability of an act and its object is maintained — *what* is grasped or understood is not reduced to the act (or acts) of understanding. However, on this view, the object is immanent to that act. It is a constituent of that temporal, subjective event which is the particular act of thinking or understanding. It is not something which can be a possible object of a plurality of acts. This means that inquiries concerning necessary truths are ultimately inquiries into individual acts and their objects.

One significant difference between these two kinds of psychologism concerns the specific mode of psychological inquiry implied by each. Humean reductive psychologism implies that inquiries into necessary truths are ultimately inquiries into empirical regularities of thought processes — they belong to what Brentano calls "empirical psychology". Subjective psychologism, however, implies that such inquiries belong to the domain of "descriptive psychology" which, by contrast, we might say

[24] These need not be the only kinds of psychologism. "Psychologism" is commonly taken to mean the first of these — Humean "reductive" psychologism. But the theories attacked by Frege and the later Husserl as being "psychologistic" — including theories consequent upon an acceptance of Brentano's account of presentations — are not of the Humean kind. A specification of why the latter are held to be "psychologistic" demands that we distinguish these two kinds of psychologism.

concerns the "structure" of a particular act of thinking. But, for all that, it is still a *psychological* theory which results from Brentano's theory of presentations insofar as the object of the inquiry is ultimately a constituent of a particular subjective psychological act.

Those aspects of Brentano's psychological thesis which lead to psychologism are his theory of presentations and the dichotomy of act and object on which it is based. In later pages we will see more clearly how these features of his descriptive psychology lead to psychologistic consequences, specifically in the case of Husserl's early work, *Philosophie der Arithmetik* (1891). In this work, Husserl attempted to construct a theory concerning the concepts and laws of arithmetic based on Brentano's theory of presentations. The result was a psychologistic theory — one which failed to establish the *logical* status of these laws and concepts.[25] We will see in the course of this later discussion, how Husserl in his subsequent works was able to avoid psychologism by dispensing with the theory of presentations, and replacing Brentano's dichotomy of act and object by the trichotomy of act, content and object.

The problem now is to see whether Brentano's insight concerning the directedness of mental phenomena can be preserved without the mentalistic conclusions of Brentano's own elaboration of this doctrine. This means abandoning not only the dualistic presuppositions which led to his doctrine of the intentional inexistence of the objects of mental phenomena, but also the "ontological approach" exemplified by the question, "What kind of existence do such objects have?" Moreover, it means abandoning the theory of presentations according to which the object to which mental acts are directed must always be something immanent to those acts. For the unwelcome consequences of this theory are, first, the exclusion of perception (what Brentano calls "outer perception") from the domain of the intentional and, second, a psychologistic theory of the "objects" of cognitive acts.

§3. *The linguistic re-formulation of Brentano's thesis of intentionality: new criteria and concerns*

In its linguistic version, intentionality is a characteristic of sentences rather than of phenomena. The peculiarities concerning

[25] See below Chapter V §1.

intentional relations and their objects are, therefore, not to be regarded as peculiarities about the status of entities or kinds of existence but, rather, as peculiarities about the kind of language that we use to *talk about* psychological phenomena. These peculiarities are expressed as criteria for the intentionality of those sentences that we use to talk about psychological phenomena.[26]

Possible non-existence of the object which, as we have seen, is Brentano's criterion for the intentionality of the mental, is re-expressed by Chisholm as a criterion for the intentionality of certain sentences about the psychological. Chisholm states his criterion as follows:

1. . . . .A simple declarative sentence is intentional if it uses a substantival expression – a name or a description – in such a way that neither the sentence nor its contradictory implies either that there is or that there isn't anything to which the substantival expression truly applies.[27]

This tells us that the sentence, "Tom is thinking of the Golden Mountain" is intentional for we cannot infer from this or its contradictory ("Tom is not thinking of the Golden Mountain") either that there is or that there is not a Golden Mountain. Sentences containing a verb like "imagining", "wishing for", "hoping for", satisfy this criterion. Sentences about physical phenomena do not satisfy this criterion: From the truth of the sentence, "Jack kicks the horse" it follows that there must exist some horse which Jack kicks. Thus, if a sentence of the form "$A \phi s Y$" is a sentence about a psychological act, then Chisholm's criterion is satisfied; if it is a sentence about a non-psychological, i.e. physical act, then Chisholm's criterion will not be satisfied.

If Brentano's thesis is to be re-formulated in such a way that intentionality becomes a feature of *all sentences* about the

---

[26] The *locus classicus* for this position is Chisholm (1957), Ch. 11. Chisholm's version of the intentionality thesis is a "re-formulation" of Brentano's theory only in a very broad sense of that term. For, as we will see in the following pages, Chisholm's account (being a thesis about language) invokes considerations from sources other than Brentano. The divergence between the two writers at this theoretical level is a consequence of the differing concerns of each: Brentano's concern was with the subject-matter of psychology; Chisholm's with the logical features of language. For a detailed discussion of Chisholm's "deviation" from Brentano, see Howarth (1980).

[27] Chisholm (1957), p. 170.

psychological, then the scope of "intentionality" must be broadened to encompass the following:

(a) sentences containing a psychological verb like "believes that", "claims that", etc., which give, in *propositional form*, the object (or, more accurately, the content) of someone's belief, claim, etc.; and

(b) sentences like "*A* sees *Y*" or "*A* remembers *Y*" which are, arguably, non-intentional by the criterion given.

To cover these sorts of cases Chisholm introduces two further criteria:

2. Any noncompound sentence which contains a propositional clause is intentional

provided that neither the sentence nor its contradictory implies either that the propositional clause is true or that it is false. . . .[28]

3. A third mark of intentionality may be described in this way. Suppose there are two names or descriptions which designate the same things and that *E* is a sentence obtained merely by separating these two names and descriptions by means of 'is identical with' . . . . Suppose that *A* is a sentence using one of those names or descriptions and that *B* is like *A* except that, where *A* uses the one, *B* uses the other. Let us say that *A* is intentional if the conjunction of *A* and *E* does not imply *B*.[29]

Chisholm's second criterion tells us that a sentence like "Tom believes that it is raining" is intentional, because we cannot infer from the sentence or its negation either that the embedded clause ("(that) it is raining") is true or is false. Sentences with a main verb like "claims that", "assumes that", "judges that", satisfy this criterion.

According to Chisholm's third criterion, if a sentence is intentional we cannot substitute co-designating expressions for one another without disturbing the truth-value of that sentence. Thus if Tully is, in fact, identical with Cicero, and it is true that "Tom believes Tully denounced Catiline", we cannot infer from the latter that "Tom believes Cicero denounced Catiline". This criterion is satisfied by sentences containing as a main verb "perceives" and

---

[28] *Ibid.*
[29] *Ibid.*, p. 171.

"remembers" as well as those containing a main verb like "knows that" which are presumed by Chisholm to be non-intentional by either the first or second criteria, respectively.

Chisholm's third criterion derives not from Brentano but from Frege. Specifically it is Frege's notion of indirect reference which is exploited here. For Frege, every expression has a sense by means of which it refers to some object. Expressions with different senses may, in fact, have the same reference. Thus, in the above example, the words "Tully" and "Cicero" have different senses although they refer to the same individual. If two expressions with different senses have the same reference they may be substituted for one another in a sentence, without disturbance to the truth-value of that sentence. Thus the truth-value of the sentence "Tully is a Roman" remains the same throughout substitutions by the word "Cicero" (which has the same reference although a different sense) within that sentence: i.e., "Cicero is a Roman". Sentences which admit substitutivity, *salva veritate*, of co-referring expressions are said to be extensional constructions.

In certain sentences substitutivity, *salva veritate*, of co-referring expressions fails. This happens in the case of sentences which form modal contexts (that is, sentences of the form, "It is necessary that . . ." or "Possibly . . .") and, as we have seen, those which form intentional contexts (sentences of the form, "*A* thinks that . . .", "*A* knows that . . ."). Such sentences are said to be non-extensional or intensional constructions. Chisholm's third criterion of non-substitutivity is, therefore, a direct borrowing of the criterion for the Fregean-derived distinction between extensional and non-extensional (intensional) constructions.

In a non-extensional construction the expression which resists substitutivity is said to have indirect or non-customary reference. This means that the expression refers not to its (customary) reference but to its sense. Frege uses the example of quotation or indirect speech to demonstrate what he means by "indirect reference". Frege says here that we may wish to speak about "the sense of some proposition, p". In this case, the customary sense of "p" becomes the reference of our discourse.

In reported speech, one talks about the sense, e.g., of another person's remarks . . . words are used indirectly or have their indirect reference. We distinguish accordingly, the customary

from the indirect reference of a word; and its customary sense
from its indirect sense . . . .[30]

In sentences containing quotation or reported speech, then, it is
the (customary) sense of the subordinate expression that the
words refer to. For this reason substitutivity, *salva veritate*, of a
co-referring expression will fail. It is only when words have their
"customary" reference that the truth-value of the sentence can be
preserved throughout substitutions. Intentional sentences form a
context of the kind in which substitutivity, *salva veritate*, fails.
Therefore, in the language of Frege, intentional sentences form a
context within which the embedded propositional clause has
indirect reference or reference to a sense.

Chisholm's second criterion can also be linked with Frege's
notion of indirect reference.[31] For Frege, the customary reference
of a sentence is the True or the False. Intentional sentences, as we
have seen, form a context in which the contained clause does not
have its customary reference. Therefore, in such contexts, the contained clause does not designate the True or the False: We cannot
infer from the sentence as a whole the truth or falsity of the
embedded clause.

Frege is clearly a significant figure in the development of a
linguistic version of Brentano's thesis of intentionality. Frege's
accounts of sense and reference and the relation between them
provide the basis for those additional criteria that must be introduced if intentionality is to be ascribed to sentences rather than to
phenomena. But before turning to a detailed examination of
Frege's contribution to contemporary debates about intentionality, it is necessary to conclude our present discussion concerning
Brentano's legacy where these debates are concerned. I shall do
this by summarising the main modifications to Brentano's original
thesis that have been effected in the course of its linguistic re-
formulation. I shall then outline two of the main advantages of
this re-formulation.

[30] Frege (1892), p. 59.

[31] Chisholm does not explicitly acknowledge that his second criterion is
traceable to Frege. The connection I am drawing here, between Chisholm's
second criterion and Frege's "indirect reference" will be spelt out more fully
when we turn to Frege's contribution to the intentionality debates in
Chapter II, below.

§4. *Advantages of the linguistic version of the intentionality thesis*

Brentano's thesis of intentionality states (1) that intentionality characterises all mental phenomena. In its linguistic version, this becomes the claim that intentionality characterises all *sentences* about psychological phenomena: Discourse about phenomena is transformed into discourse about sentences. (2) Brentano's statement that "no physical phenomenon manifests anything like (intentionality)" is re-formulated as the claim that intentionality is absent in sentences that we use to talk about non-psychological phenomena. (3) Brentano says of the object to which a mental activity is directed that it is not to be understood as "a thing" (i.e., as a "reality"), and he explains this by saying that it enjoys "intentional in-existence". In the linguistic re-formulation, the notion of "intentional in-existence" can be dropped because the possible non-existence of the object can be expressed in terms of the "behaviour" of certain sentences that we use to talk about psychological activities, *viz.*, that such sentences do not carry existential implication: From the truth of the sentence, "A thinks of Y" we cannot infer "$(\exists x)\, A$ thinks of x."[32]

This brings us to the first major advantage of the linguistic re-formulation: Its avoidance of the twin evils of (a) introducing a Meinongian ontology, and (b) postulating intra-mental entities.

Questions about the existence or non-existence of an object of thinking, wishing, etc., become questions about the way in which certain expressions may succeed or fail in picking out some object. Certain sentences about psychological activities — those of the form "$A\ \phi$'s Y" — are formed by a predicate and two referring expressions. The expression which designates the object of the activity may fail to refer to anything, as in "A thinks of Pegasus". In this respect, an expression which designates a non-existent object of thought is like any other expression such as "the present king of France" or "the Golden Mountain" which, although meaningful, does not succeed in picking out any existing object. However in cases such as these there is no need to provide a "referent"

---

[32] In this particular example, the quantifier must be read objectually — i.e., in such a way that the quantified formula is true if there exists some object which satisfies that formula.

such as a Meinongian non-entity, an intra-mental object or a mental representation for a sentence containing the expression to be *about*. Such postulates are not necessary for an understanding of how such expressions function meaningfully in sentences. For example, Russell deals with such expressions in terms of his theory of descriptions: A referring expression which fails to pick out anything can be re-analysed as a predicate, so that a sentence containing that expression turns out to be false. Questions about the non-existence of an object referred to thus become questions about the truth or falsity of sentences containing a referring expression. Or, alternatively, on Frege's theory, these troublesome expressions can be dealt with by appeal to the notion of sense.

When the object of a psychological act *does* exist, as in the case expressed by the sentence, "Tom is thinking of Mrs. Thatcher", then the expression "Mrs. Thatcher" does succeed in picking out some real existing object. And this means that what is referred to by the words "Mrs. Thatcher" in that sentence is that existing individual that one might also hit or kick. The individual picked out in the case of a genuine referring expression is not some entity in addition to "the real thing". Thus the claim that mental phenomena can succeed in achieving objective reference (*Thesis I*) seems to present no special problems, for "objective reference" can be explicated linguistically – by appeal to the notion of linguistic reference, rather than to modes or kinds of existence.

One consequence of admitting this possibility of objective reference in the case of intentional acts is that the class of "the mental" (of which intentionality is the mark) need not be restricted to those acts which constitute a purely mental relation or which are directed to purely mental objects. We can include amongst "the mental", acts like thinking, wishing, hoping for some *existing Y*, and we can also include acts designated by part-behavioural terms, like "aiming at" and "worshipping". Even more significantly, we can include within the domain of the intentional what Brentano calls "outer perception". "Outer perception" is the sense of perception which implies that there exists some real physical object which is percieved. Thus "the mental" which is talked about in sentences that are intentional is a much broader domain than Brentano's domain of "the mental". To indicate the broadening of this domain, I shall follow Chisholm in using the word "psychological" to designate those phenomena talked about in intentional sentences. What is significant about extending the class of phenomena which are designated "intentional" in this way is that it seems to undercut the kind of dualism which led to Brentano's exclusion of "outer perception" from the domain of the intentional; mental acts can succeed in achieving objective reference – reference to physical objects – and, therefore, objects of thought can no longer be regarded as immanent to the act of thinking.

A second major advantage of the linguistic formulation of the intentionality thesis is that it allows us to explicate an ambiguity in the phrase "object of thought". Prior[33] points out that "object of thought" may be taken to mean "*what* is thought", or it may mean "what is thought *about*". If Tom thinks that snow is white, we can ask "*What* does Tom think?" The answer, "that snow is white", gives us the *content* of Tom's thought. Or we can ask "What does Tom think *about*?" The answer, "snow", gives the *object* of Tom's thought which, in a sentence of this form, is the subject of the proposition giving the content of thought. (There is also a third sense of "object of thought", *viz.*, given that Tom is thinking about some object, we can always ask what Tom thinks *of it*. But we can, for the moment, postpone discussion of this.) Brentano, in his formulation of the intentionality thesis, conflates these two senses of "objects of thought" – desired objects and propositions judged are alike classified as intentionally inexistent *objects*.[34]

According to Chisholm intentionality is a feature of "those sentences we use to talk about psychological phenomena". Now the "psychological phenomena" that we talk about might comprise the content of someone's thought or the object of someone's thought or both. Objects of thought are usually talked about in

---

[33] Prior (1971), pp. 3–4.

[34] Elsewhere, [Brentano (1874) Book II, ch. vii and, more explicitly, in Brentano (1911)], Brentano does distinguish between content and object in order to show that the *content* of e.g., an act of judging can never be made an *object* of mental reference. Thus, if I judge that a centaur does not exist, it is "a centaur" which is the object of my judging, and not a centaur's existence or non-existence. This means that, for Brentano, the intentionality of acts like judging, affirming, denying, etc., which have propositional content consists, ultimately, in a relation to the *object* judged, etc.

sentences of direct-object form: "*X* thinks of *Y*". Contents of thought are usually talked about in sentences of propositional form: "*X* thinks that *p*". Sentences which are explicitly of one of these forms can often be re-expressed in the other form. One case of this we have already seen: Tom's thinking *that* snow is white can be re-expressed as a sentence about the object of Tom's thought, in which case it has the direct-object form, "Tom thinks *of* snow". Conversely, if we wish to talk about the content of thought in Jack's thinking *of* Pegasus, we do so by expressing Jack's thought in a sentence which has propositional form — "Jack thinks *that* Pegasus φ's".

The peculiarities of sentences of one form are different in some important respects from the peculiarities of sentences of the other form. For example, the object of a sentence of direct-object form may sometimes be abstract; but the content of a sentence of propositional form is always abstract. This difference is sometimes expressed by saying that the object of an intentional sentence of the first form is an "intentional object" while the content of an intentional sentence of the second form is an "intensional object" — a proposition or meaning. The content of a sentence, that is, a proposition, is not *prima facie* the kind of thing about which existential questions can be raised.[35] Propositions are vehicles of truth or falsity. This suggests that different modes of analysis are appropriate to the different kinds of sentences that are used to talk about the psychological. For example, the psychological verb in a sentence of direct-object form — "*X* thinks of *Y*" — is a predicate flanked by two referring expressions. Taken this way, a sentence of direct-object form might be analysed in terms of a relation between the individuals designated by the subject and object expressions. However, there are difficulties with the attempt to assimilate sentences of propositional form to this mode of analysis. If "believes" in a sentence of the form, "*X* believes that *p*" is interpreted as a relational predicate, it is not clear how the content of the belief — "that *p*" — is to be analysed as one of the terms of a relation. In Chapter III, §1, we will see some of the problems arising from Russell's attempts to analyse a sentence like "*X* believes that *p*" in terms of (a) a relation between *X* and the "*constituents*" of the proposition believed, and (b) a

---

[35] We will see in Chapter V, below, some of the reasons for denying this.

relation between X and the *fact* that is expressed by the proposition.

A more fruitful approach to sentences of propositional form has been to analyse them in terms of operators or functions. This means that the verb, "thinks", in a sentence of the form "X thinks that p" is treated not as a predicate which forms a sentence from two names, but as part of an operator, "X-thinks-that", which forms a sentence from another sentence, that is, from the sentence giving the content of the thought or the belief. A sentence about the psychological which has propositional form can now be analysed as a *function of the proposition* expressing the content of the thought – $F(p)$.

The availability of this functional mode of analysis in the case of sentences giving the content of thought means that we can appeal to the *intensionality* of language in characterising the *intentionality* of these sentences about the psychological. We have already seen that Chisholm's criterion of non-substitutivity is the Fregean-derived principle for the intensionality of language. Intensional constructions are those which fail to satisfy the criteria for extensionality. The criteria for extensionality can be stated in terms of functions. Prior states these criteria as follows:

> To say that a function F of propositions, properties, relations, etc., is an *extensional* one is to say that is satisfies the appropriate member of the series of formulae which begins as follows:
>
> (i) $(p)(q): p \equiv q . \supset . F(p) \equiv F(q)$
> (ii) $(\phi)(\psi): (x)(\phi x \equiv \psi x) . \supset . F(\phi) \equiv F(\psi)$
> (iii) $(\phi)(\psi): (x)(y)(\phi xy \equiv \psi xy) . \supset . F(\phi) \equiv F(\psi)$
> (iv) $(\phi)(\psi): (x)(y)(z)(\phi xyz \equiv \psi xyz) . \supset . F(\phi) \equiv F(\psi)$.
>
> ... To say that a function F is a *non-extensional* or *intensional* one is to say that it does not satisfy the appropriate member of this series.[36]

Intensional functions, then, are not truth-functions: the truth-value of the argument does not determine the truth of the function. The truth-value of an intensional function is disturbed when the sentence which is its argument is replaced by a sentence

---

[36] Prior (1968), p. 91.

equivalent in truth-value but expressing a different proposition. This means that differences in the propositions expressed by sentences which are materially equivalent are significant where the determination of the truth-value of certain functions is concerned. Propositional identity is not the same thing as material equivalence. So, by admitting intensional functions, we thereby recognise a significant difference between the proposition expressed by a sentence (what we might call the "meaning" or, in Frege's termi-nology, the "sense" of the expression) and the truth-value of the sentence (what Frege would call the "reference" of the sentence).

However, in recognising this difference, we thereby introduce "intensional objects" — for Prior, these are the propositions, properties and relations which occur as arguments of an intensional function. In Frege's case, intensional objects are called "intensions", that is, senses or meanings conceived of as abstract entities.[37] A theory of language which admits intensional constructions is one which thereby admits intensional objects. Such a theory is *known as an intensionalist theory*.

We can now see how an intensionalist theory of language is relevant to the intentionality of thought when the latter is expressed in terms of criteria governing the sentences we use to talk about the *content* of thought. If "the psychological" is talked about in a sentence of propositional form — i.e., one giving the content of thought — then that sentence can be analysed as an intensional function. This mode of analysis ensures that Chisholm's second and third criteria for intentionality are satisfied: The third criterion for intentionality — non-substitutivity — is of course automatically satisfied, for this *is* the principle of intensionality. But furthermore, intensional functions are not truth-functions therefore, if an intentional sentence is analysed as an intensional function, Chisholm's second criterion (non-implication of truth or falsity) is satisfied. This criterion tells us that the truth of an intentional sentence, for example, "Tom believes that snow is pink", does not depend upon the truth of the sentence which

---

[37] Prior resists this identification of "intensional objects" with "intensions" by admitting non-nominal quantification, thereby treating "intensional objects" not as entities named by abstract nouns (intensions), but as expressions which perform e.g., an adverbial or adjectival role. This is Prior's way of responding to Quine's critique of "intensions". These are questions to be discussed in Chapter V, below.

states the content of Tom's thought, *viz.*, "snow is pink". It depends, rather, on whether the proposition expressed by that sentence is *believed by Tom.*

If we appeal to the intensionality of language in order to explicate the notion of intentionality, then we can specify what we mean by the "content" of thought. Differences in the content of thought are significant where the truth-value of intentional sentences is concerned: There is a difference between Tom's believing that snow is pink and Tom's believing that snow is purple, even though the sentences which describe Tom's belief in each case are materially equivalent. The difference, here, is a difference in the *content* of each belief. If we appeal to an intensionalist theory of language we can perserve this difference, for, on this kind of theory, propositional identity is not the same thing as material equivalence. The content of Tom's thought in the sentence, "Tom believes that snow is pink" is the proposition expressed by the sentence, "snow is pink". This proposition is the argument of an intensional function — i.e., it is an intensional object. The *content* of thought is, therefore, to be understood as an *intensional object.*

For Frege intensional objects are intensions — meanings conceived of as abstract entities. On Frege's account, then, a theory of language which admits intensional constructions thereby admits intensions which in turn means a commitment to a particular notion of meaning. We have seen how, for Frege, expressions which occur within intensional contexts do not have their customary reference but refer, instead, to a sense. Senses are, therefore, intensions — i.e., meanings.

By way of summarising the second major advantage of the linguistic approach to intentionality, we can re-state the following points. We can distinguish between objects and contents of thought in virtue of the different modes of analysis appropriate to the form of sentence we use to talk about each. Sentences which give the object of thought are to be analysed in terms of the success or failure of reference in the case of the words which give the object of thought. Sentences which give the content of thought are to be analysed as intensional functions in which case the content of thought can be understood as an intensional object or meaning. For Frege intentional objects or intensions are senses. The notion of intentionality can, therefore, be explicated by appeal to Frege's notion of sense.

SENSE, REFERENCE AND SEMANTICAL FRAMEWORKS

§1. *Frege's theory of sense*

The transition from talk about the intentionality of phenomena to talk about the intentionality of sentences introduces new criteria and considerations which are not to be found in Brentano's original formulation. These are Chisholm's second and third criteria which, by invoking notions of truth and falsity and the notion of linguistic reference, are applicable to sentences rather than to phenomena. The acknowledged source of Chisholm's third criterion — non-substitutivity — is Frege's notion of indirect reference: reference to the sense of an expression.

An understanding of what Frege means by indirect reference (and, hence, an understanding of how Chisholm's third criterion is to be exploited) requires that we examine Frege's notions of "sense" (*Sinn*) and "reference" (*Bedeutung*), and their relationship to one another. Frege introduces his essay, "On Sense and Reference",[1] by considering the relation of identity which can be expressed differently in "$a = a$" and in true statements of the form "$a = b$". The two statements differ in cognitive value. The first, "$a = a$", holds *a priori*; the second, "$a = b$", is something whose truth can be discovered. The problem of identity had already been dealt with by Frege in the *Begriffsschrift*[2] in relation to questions concerning a logical calculus. But it is clearly questions of an epistemological kind which are relevant to the discussion of

---

[1] Frege (1892).
[2] Frege's *Begriffsschrift, eine der arithmetischen nachgebildete Formelsprache des reinen Denkens* (Halle, 1879).

identity in "On Sense and Reference". The general problem, for
Frege, is this: How are we to understand the relation of identity so
that we can acknowledge a difference in the cognitive value of
those statements in which a judgement of identity can be
expressed? If identity is taken to be a relation between the objects
that the names "a" and "b" designate (or, more accurately, the
relation of an object to itself), then this difference would be
masked — the statement "$a = b$", if true, would be no different
from the *a priori* judgement, "$a = a$". On the other hand, there are
problems with asserting that identity is a relation between the
signs themselves (the view which Frege had earlier assumed in the
Begriffsschrift). On this view, the signs "a" and "b" are related
only insofar as they designate the same object. But it is an arbitrary
matter that we decide to use these signs to designate the same
thing and so the statement "$a = b$" would be a relation between
our arbitrarily chosen "modes of designation".[3] Here, "$a = a$"
would be no different from "$a = b$" (if true). This way of understanding the identity relation is inadequate to tell us how statements of the form "$a = b$" contain "valuable extensions of our
knowledge".[4]

Frege states that the difference in the cognitive value of the two
true identity statements, "$a = a$" and "$a = b$", corresponds to "a
difference in the mode of presentation of that which is presented".[5]
Frege illustrates this with an example from geometry: If a, b, c, be
lines connecting the vertices of a triangle with the midpoints of
the opposite sides, the point of intersection of b and c is the same
as the point of intersection of a and b. Here we have different
designations (i.e. names) for the same point — "the point of intersection of a and b" and "the point of intersection of b and c".
These different designations for the same point indicate the different modes of presentation.[6] Frege concludes from this that in
addition to the object designated with a sign — what Frege calls
the *reference* of the sign — there is connected a *sense* which
contains the mode of presentation of the object. Thus different

[3] Frege (1892), p. 57.
[4] *Ibid.*, p. 56.
[5] *Ibid.*, p. 57.
[6] *Ibid.*

names, like "the morning star" and "the evening star" which have the same reference, have different senses.

Frege begins by discussing the sense and reference of names. By "name" or "sign" he means "any designation representing a proper name, which thus has as its reference a definite object . . . but not a concept or relation . . . ."[7] A proper name may be a word or combination of words. The sense of a name is what is grasped in common by those who speak and understand a language:

> The sense of a proper name is grasped by everybody who is sufficiently familiar with the language or totality of designations to which it belongs . . . .[8]

But grasping the sense of a name cannot consist in knowing what the reference of the name is, for grasping the sense "serves to illuminate only a single aspect of the reference supposing it to have one".[9] The reference of a name (when there is one) is, for Frege, only given one-sidedly. Frege adds:

> Comprehensive knowledge of the reference would require us to be able to say immediately whether any given sense belongs to it. To such knowledge we never attain.[10]

But although to every sign (i.e., name) there corresponds a sense, in grasping a sense "one is not certainly assured of a reference".[11] Frege gives as examples the expressions "the celestial body most distant from the earth", which has a sense but only doubtfully a reference, and "the least rapidly convergent series", which also has a sense but no reference. This shows that we can understand or meaningfully use names which have no reference (or for which a reference is doubtful).

If our interest in language is motivated by "cognitive concerns" — concerns relating to the understanding of a language — then, according to Frege, it is necessary to connect with names not just

---

[7] *Ibid.*

[8] *Ibid.*, pp. 57–8.

[9] *Ibid.*, p. 58.

[10] *Ibid.* Thiel (1968) p. 86, points out that this remark of Frege's had led to the charge of specticism. We will see in Chapter VI, by comparing Frege's account of the "one-sidedness" of knowledge with Husserl's account of the perspectival nature of perception, that specticism need not be implied by Frege's account of the relation of sense to reference.

[11] Frege (1892), p. 58.

a reference but, in addition, a sense. By appeal to the notion of sense we can recognise the difference in the cognitive value of different names which are used to refer to the same object (which have the same reference); we can account for the fact that names which lack a reference can be understood or used meaningfully. These are two considerations which must be accounted for if our interests are cognitive ones. In order to account for these considerations we must replace the dichotomy of

sign (name)   —   referent (object)

with the trichotomy of

sign (name)   —   sense   —   referent (object).[12]

We can see the significance of this replacement when we turn to Frege's theses concerning sense:

1. To every sign there is correlated a sense, although there need not be a reference

There can be no signs (i.e., names) which lack a sense; every sign which has a reference necessarily has a sense: "Every grammatically well-formed expression representing a proper name always has a sense . . .".[13] But every expression, although it has a sense, does not necessarily have a reference: ". . . but this is not to say that to the sense there also corresponds a reference".[14]

2. Senses are objective

Frege's remarks suggest that there are three different ways of characterising the objectivity of sense:

(i) First, there is an ontological characterisation which follows from Frege's statement that "thoughts are senses of sentences".[15] For Frege, the thought expressed by a sentence is the bearer of

---

[12] Føllesdal (1972), p. 421.

[13] Frege (1892), p. 58.

[14] *Ibid*.

[15] Frege (1918), p. 4. Frege adds that this is not to say that the sense of every sentence is a thought — it is only assertoric sentences whose sense is a thought.

truth or falsity. Thoughts belong neither to the "inner realm" of private and subjective ideas nor to the "outer realm" of material perceptible objects, but to a "third realm", whose objects share certain features with those of the other two realms:

> A third realm must be recognised. Anything belonging to this realm has it in common with ideas that it cannot be perceived by the senses, but has it in common with things that it does not need an owner so as to belong to the contents of his consciousness . . . .[16]

This ontological characterisation of the thought can be re-expressed as a semantic characterisation of sense by saying that senses are abstract entities or intensions.[17] But there is another way of identifying sense with the thought, whereby we can assert the objectivity of sense without commitment to ontological realms:[18]

(ii) The sense of a sign is that which is grasped by those who speak and understand a common language. It is not a subjective idea or image. Frege says, ". . . the sign's sense . . . may be the common property of many and therefore is not part or a mode of the individual mind".[19] Frege draws the analogy of the moon as seen through a telescope. The moon itself is comparable to the reference, the subjective retinal image analogous to the subjective idea, but the optical image projected by the glass, which is only a one-sided view of the moon but is nonetheless observable by many, is comparable to the sense. In the case of a sentence it is the thought which is the sense. Frege here stresses that by "a thought" he means "not the subjective performance of thinking but its objective content which is capable of being the common property of several thinkers".[20] Sense or the thought is objective in that it

---

[16] *Ibid.*, p. 17.

[17] Whether the notion of "intension" which plays a role in formal semantics — e.g., Church (1951) — is a notion which can be dissociated from ontological considerations is a question which will be raised in Chapter IV.

[18] This is not to say that Frege's "ontological approach" is to be dismissed. That this approach is to be taken seriously in its own right is evident from recent studies in the field of ontology. See Angelelli (1967); Thiel (1968) VIII; Smith (1978).

[19] Frege (1892), p. 59.

[20] *Ibid.*, p. 62n.

is the "common property" of language users and not a private, subjective idea.

(iii) Finally, senses are objective insofar as they can be referred to — i.e., they are possible referents. In indirect or reported speech an expression is used to refer in a non-customary way: such an expression does not have its customary reference but refers instead to a sense. Senses can be referred to. Senses therefore can be said to be objective to the extent that reference is objective.

3. Sense is not the same thing as reference

(i) A sign (which necessarily has a sense) need not have a reference, as in the case of the name "the least rapidly convergent series". For Frege the sense of a sentence depends upon the sense of its parts; the reference of a sentence depends on the reference of its parts. A sentence containing a name which has no reference (or a name whose reference is doubtful) has a sense, for example, "Odysseus was set ashore at Ithaca while sound asleep". It is only when we are concerned with the truth-value — for Frege, the reference — of the sentence, that we advance from the sense of the name to its reference.[21]

(ii) The same reference may correspond to different signs with different senses although the converse does not hold — signs which have the same sense have the same reference. We have seen how this is so in the case of the different true identity statements, "$a = a$" and "$a = b$", where difference of sense is said to be difference in the cognitive value of each statement.

(iii) The sense of a sign is the mode in which the reference of that sign is presented — sense is always "one-sided". Difference in sense is therefore difference in the mode of presentation or of the aspect under which the reference is known.

Sense, then, is contrastable with reference. But it is not in opposition to reference, for:

4. Sense is a determinant of reference

There is always something — viz., sense — in virtue of which we grasp what it is that a sign refers to. Therefore reference — the

---

[21] *Ibid.*, p. 63.

relation between a sign and its referent — is a relation which is mediated by sense. Reference is a function of the sense of an expression. Signs with different senses may have the same reference although the converse does not hold. It follows that the sense of a sign is not a function of — i.e., is not uniquely determined by — its reference.

Frege's semantical framework, then, is a three-levelled one consisting of

sign — sense — referent

By a "three-levelled semantical framework",[22] here, I mean one which entails all four of the above features concerning "sense". In summary, it is a framework which entails that

1. every expression necessarily has a sense but only contingently a reference;
2. senses are objective — i.e., are possible referents;
3. the sense and reference of an expression are not one and the same thing;
4. sense is a determinant of reference.

These theses jointly comprise Frege's "theory of sense".

We can now sketch an outline of the way that a theory of intentionality might appeal to Frege's notion of sense. *Thesis I* tells us that mental phenomena can succeed in achieving objective reference. Consistent with the linguistic approach to intentionality, we are to understand "objective reference", here, in terms of linguistic reference — the relation between a sign and its referent. If linguistic reference is explicated against Frege's three-levelled semantical framework, then this relation is one that is mediated by sense. Moreover, the Fregean framework admits signs, with senses, which do not refer to anything: Signs can be meaningful even though they have no reference. In terms of the Fregean semantical framework, an account of possible success in achieving reference *or* of the absence of reference will be one which invokes the notion of sense.

Although it is the notion of sense which is fundamental here it is

[22]*Cf.* Küng (1972). Although I am making use of Küng's terminology — "three-levelled semantical framework" — I am exploiting this notion in a quite different way. It is not just the structure of this framework that I designate by this term but, in addition, the content. According to my usage of the term the level of sense is necessarily Fregean sense as characterised here.

important to identify that aspect of the notion of "reference" which is relevant to a theory of sense. We must ask: What are we to understand by "reference" as that which is mediated by sense? Frege uses the word *Bedeutung* in three different ways: for the relation between the sign and the object which it stands for; for the fact of a sign's standing for a particular object; for the object itself that the sign stands for.[23] The last of these is usually called the "referent". Where a theory of sense is concerned, it is primarily the first of these — the relation between sign and referent which concerns us. Talk about the sense of an expression is talk about the way in which a sign relates to some object; a concern with sense indicates a concern with the cognitive aspects of language so that the significant problems are those arising from the observations that (a) different signs (with different senses) may be connected with the same reference; and (b) a sign may be meaningful even though it has no reference. Both of these observations raise problems about reference as the relation between signs and objects that they stand for.

But there is, we might say, a further dimension to Frege's notion of reference according to which reference consists in the fact of a word's (or symbol's) standing for some object. This aspect of reference belongs to the sphere of Frege's "logical concerns" — the sphere of his formal semantics. Within this sphere of concerns a particular interpretation of the sentences of predicate logic fixes the reference of the non-logical constants, and truth-values are assigned to those sentences on the basis of the interpretation.[24]

Now, the theory of sense tells us how the association of word (or symbol) and object is effected. Accordingly, in a theory of sense, we cannot assume the *fact* of a word's standing for some object, for it is precisely this relation between a word and its referent that a theory of sense is designed to explain.

Dummett makes this point when he states that "reference is not an ingredient of meaning".[25] Dummett describes a theory of meaning as a theory of what a person knows when he understands

[23] Dummett (1973), pp. 93—4. Dummett points out there is no confusion of these uses in Frege's writings.

[24] *Ibid.*, pp. 89—90.

[25] *Ibid.*, p. 91.

an expression. This in turn involves an account of how language functions and what it is that language does. Dummett shows the shortcomings of a formal semantic notion of reference in this respect: Semantics tells us, solely in terms of reference, *that* a symbol is to be associated with a referent, but it doesn't tell us *how* this association is established. "Where the semantic account is lacking is that it does not go far enough back; it postulates an association between each primitive symbol and its appropriate referent, but it does not tell us how this association is established. For the purposes of logic this is unnecessary; for the purposes of meaning, it is essential.[26]

The thesis, "reference is not an ingredient of meaning", amounts to the claim that our understanding of an expression can never consist merely in our associating something in the world with that expression. There must be "some particular *means* by which this association is effected, the knowledge of which constitutes (our) grasp of its sense. It follows that, upon occasion, the same thing can be associated with two different words or expressions as their referent, the association being effected by different means in the two cases, and the two words thus having different senses in spite of having the same reference."[27]

A theory of sense is tied to a theory of understanding. In the case of our understanding a proper name, for example, there must be something in virtue of which we grasp what the referent of that name is. This "something in virtue of which . . ." is the *sense*[28] of the name. The sense of a proper name cannot therefore consist in its having the reference that it has — cannot consist in *the fact* of that name's standing for the individual which is its referent. For, if this were so, no true identity statement could be informative; there would be no difference in the cognitive value of co-referring

[26] *Ibid.*, p. 93.

[27] *Ibid.*

[28] This is not to say that a grasp of the complete sense is necessary for understanding. Frege remarks in a footnote (Frege (1892), p. 58n) that opinions as to the sense of a proper name such as "Aristotle" may differ, but that such variations may be tolerated so long as the reference remains the same. Consistent with Frege's statement that "to every expression . . . there should certainly correspond a definite sense", (p. 58), we must interpret this to mean that, on occasions, a partial grasp of the sense of a name is sufficient for our understanding what that name refers to.

expressions like "the morning star" and "the evening star" which have different senses and, therefore, no accounting for the fact that we may come to learn the truth of an identity statement. If the sense of a proper name consisted in the name's having the reference that it has, then my understanding of the name would consist solely in knowing what object is associated with a word, so that understanding two names with the same reference would consist in knowing the truth of an identity statement connecting them so that this statement of identity would not, therefore, be informative. Understanding – grasping the sense of – a name means connecting the name with a particular way of identifying the object which is its referent. Thus different names which have the same referent are connected with different ways of identifying the object which is the referent of each.

The notion of reference that enters into a theory of sense or understanding (as when we say reference is a function of the sense), is not to be interpreted as the fact of a word's association with some object. For this is to beg the very question that a theory of sense is (at least in part) designed to answer – *viz.*, how *does* a word relate to some object which is its referent?

Standard interpretations of Frege's notions of sense and reference do not observe the kind of distinction I am emphasising here, between those aspects of reference relating to Frege's "logical concerns" (reference as the fact of a word's standing for some object), on the one hand, and those aspects relating to his theory of sense (reference as a function of sense), on the other. Russell, for example, has exploited just those aspects relating to Frege's logical concerns – reference as the fact of a word's association with some object. Russell then goes on to combine these aspects of reference with his own Cartesian-based epistemology with its distinction between knowlege by acquaintance and knowledge by description. Fregean "sense" is then associated with knowledge by description, while "reference" is associated with knowledge by acquaintance and comes to be construed in terms of access to the "real". Later chapters will show in some detail what Russell's theory of reference consists in and how, as a result of accepting this notion of reference, Fregean sense is necessarily distorted.[29]

---

[29] See Appendix A.

What our present deliberations show is that, when reference is characterised against Frege's three-levelled semantical framework, we must put aside those aspects of Fregean reference which relate to his logical concerns in order to examine how a relation between a sign and its referent is effected.

Thus our understanding of "reference", here, depends in a very crucial way upon the notion of sense. Fregean sense has both a cognitive and semantic dimension.[30] Senses are what is grasped in cognitive activities such as understanding or knowing the meaning of an expression (2(ii) above). Difference in the senses of expressions which have the same reference is explained as a difference in the cognitive value of those expressions (3(ii) above). Senses are therefore *mind-related* in the same way that cognitive activities such as understanding or knowing the meaning of some term are mind-related. The semantic dimension of sense concerns the role assigned to sense in a theory about the relationship between language and the world, or about the relationship between particular expressions of a language and the way in which they serve to pick out or identify objects in the world. Frege tells us that sense is *the means by which* this relationship is effected (4 above). Sense is therefore at once (a) mind-related, and (b) the vehicle of reference.

Although Frege's theory tells us *that* sense is both of these things, it provides no account of *how* sense can be at once mind-related and a vehicle of reference. The shortcomings of Frege's theory of sense in this respect will become conspicuous in Chapter V, when we see how, in the absence of Frege's provision of a theory about the relation of mind to meaning, certain critics have imputed to him a mentalistic theory of meaning. It is in response to this kind of criticism that I shall be urging in Chapter VI that Fregean sense be regarded as an "intentional" notion – a notion backed by Husserl's phenomenological theory of the way in which meaning is at once "mind-related" and a vehicle of reference.

---

[30] The notion of "semantic dimension" here must be clearly distinguished from the notion of "semantic" which occurs in the expression, "formal semantic theory" or "formal semantics".

§2. *Russell's theory of names*

For Russell names are the basic vehicles of reference. But contrary to the Fregean account of names as signs which possess a sense and possibly a reference, names, for Russell, refer in the absence of sense. Russell's account of reference is set against a two-levelled semantical framework consisting of:

sign   —   referent.

The relation between

name   —   bearer,

which, for Russell, is fundamental to this framework, is a relation which is unmediated by sense. Names are signs which necessarily have a reference but no sense.

Without the level of sense, the only genuine referring expressions[31] are those for which there exists some object (a referent): There can be no signs (i.e., referring expressions) which do not refer to anything; the only expressions which are names are those which pick out some object, and they do this without the mediation of sense.

But here we strike immediate problems. Certain expressions which Frege calls "names" do not seem to be accommodated by the Russellian framework:

1. Certain ordinary proper names, such as "Pegasus", which are meaningful, have no bearer. The Russellian framework precludes the possibility of saying that these are signs which have a sense but no reference.
2. Certain expressions, such as "the present queen of England" or "the present king of France" (which, for Frege are included within the class of names), are meaningful regardless of whether or not there exists anything to which they refer. In terms of the Fregean framework, we can say of such expressions that they necessarily possess a sense but only contingently a reference.

Russell's way of dealing with these seemingly recalcitrant expressions is to exclude them from the category of names. Russell distinguishes between names and descriptions. Names necessarily

---

[31] That is, what Frege calls "signs".

have a reference; descriptions only contingently apply to some particular individual. Vacuous "names", such as "Pegasus", for which there exists no reference, and denoting phrases, such as "the present queen of England", for which it is only a contingent matter that there does exist a reference, belong not to the category of names, but to the category of descriptions. This means that a sentence containing any of these expressions as subject-term is to be analysed according to Russell's theory of descriptions.[32] Russell's celebrated example of "the present king of France" provides the model for this analysis. The sentence, "The present king of France is wise", is meaningful despite the fact that there exists nothing which is denoted by the subject-term, and hence nothing to which the predicate "is wise" can be truly applied. For Russell this sentence is to be analysed as the conjunction, "There is something such that it is a king of France and there is nothing other than this individual such that it is a king of France, and this individual is wise." When either of the first two conjuncts is false, the resulting sentence is false. Expressions which only contingently refer to some individual – i.e., denoting expressions which are meaningful regardless of whether they refer to anything – are thus to be analysed not as names, but as descriptions. Ordinary proper names like "Pegasus", which do not refer to anything, are to be treated as disguised descriptions and submitted to the same analysis.

Names, as contrasted with descriptions, *necessarily* refer. We must ask: What semantic property (or properties) do names possess such that we can mark them off as expressions which necessarily refer? Or, in other words, what is distinctive about the relation between a name and its bearer as contrasted with the relation between a description and some object to which it contingently applies? To answer this question, we must turn to one of the important influences on Russell's distinction between names and descriptions – Mill's theory of Proper names.

Mill[33] distinguishes between connotative and non-connotative terms. General names (such as common nouns and adjectives) are connotative – they give the attributes that an object may possess. We can use them meaningfully without knowing what object or

[32] Russell (1905).
[33] Mill (1843).

objects they apply to. What they apply to forms no part of their meaning. Singular names may or may not be connotative. A connotative singular name is an expression like "the president of France in 1982". We can use such an expression meaningfully without knowing what it applies to or whether it applies to anything. But when such a term does apply, it applies uniquely to the individual which possesses the attributes that the term can then be said to connote. Non-connotative singular names are proper names like "M. Mitterand". Proper names are "meaningless marks" — they have denotation but no connotation. Proper names in themselves carry no information about the bearer of the name. They do not connote any attributes whereby we might recognise something as the bearer of the name. They serve to identify directly the individual that they denote. We may, of course, have information about the bearer of the name (about the individual, M. Mitterand), but this information forms no part of the meaning of the Proper name and plays no part in the actual use of name in a sentence. The understanding of a Proper name, therefore, involves a "direct" association of word and object (i.e., name and bearer). "Direct" here means "in the absence of connotation". Knowing the attributes of the object associated with a Proper name is not a determinant in our understanding of what a Proper name denotes.

Mill's distinction between non-connotative and connotative singular names is re-expressed by Russell as the distinction between names and descriptions. As with Mill, the distinction is based on the way in which expressions relate to their objects. Names are those expressions which serve to pick out some particular individual in the absence of any descriptive information (i.e., non-connotatively); denoting phrases, such as "the present queen of England", serve to pick out some individual by means of descriptive information (connotatively) — they are therefore to be analysed as descriptions. Mill's concern was to classify (singular) names — that is, words which *are* associated with some object[34] — on the basis of the *way* in which different kinds of names relate to their objects — connotatively or non-connotatively. But Russell's concerns were with the possible non-existence of the denotation

---

[34] "Names . . . shall always be spoken of in this work as the names of things themselves". Mill (1843), p. 14.

of expressions we use to refer: ". . . a name has got to name something or it is not a name, and if there is no such person as Romulus there cannot be a name for that person who is not there . . ."[35] His problems were those relating to expressions like "the present king of France" for which there exists no denotation. Hence, what is significant for Russell is that Mill's distinction is one concerning the necessity or contingency of there being some object to which the different kinds of expressions are related.

Because for Russell names must refer to existing things, Mill's distinction can be usefully exploited in the case of genuine referring expressions. Within the class of expressions which refer we can distinguish between names which pick out their object in the absence of descriptive information (non-connotatively) and descriptions which do so by means of descriptive information (connotatively). But, for Russell, what is significant about those expressions which refer connotatively is the fact that they can be meaningful regardless of whether or not there exists anything to which they uniquely apply. This is not so in the case of a name. A name can *only* be "meaningful" (i.e., be the subject of a meaningful sentence) if there exists something to which it refers. The existence of the bearer of a name must be *guaranteed*, otherwise there would be no difference between names and descriptions in respect of the *necessity* of there being a referent in the case of a name. Only things whose existence is guaranteed can be bearers of a name. This is not equivalent to the claim that the bearers of names have necessary existence. Although the latter claim may be one way of stating what the "guarantee of existence" consists in, it is not Russell's way. But in what sense is existence guaranteed? For Russell's answer to this question, we must turn to his Cartesian-derived epistemological theory, with its distinction between knowledge by acquaintance and knowledge by description. In this way we will see how, for Russell, the necessity pertaining to names — which we express by saying that a name cannot fail to refer — is underpinned by an epistemological theory concerning our knowlege of the object which is the bearer of the name.

Russell's epistemological theory is based on the Cartesian

[35] Russell (1918), p. 243.

distinction between corrigible and incorrigible knowledge.[36] The naming relation (Mill's "denoting" relation) consists in the "direct" association of word and object. Understanding a name consists in knowing "directly" what particular individual that term picks out. We have seen how the "directness" of the association of a name and its bearer consists in the absence of descriptive mediation (it is a non-connotative relation). Similarly, the "directness" of our knowledge of the object picked out by a name means knowledge that is unmediated by descriptive information. Russell calls such knowledge "knowledge by direct acquaintance". By this Russell means Cartesian *incorrigible* knowledge: "Whatever we are acquainted with must be something; we may draw wrong inferences from our acquaintance, but the acquaintance itself cannot be deceptive".[37] Descriptions do not give us knowledge by direct acquaintance about the object(s) to which they apply. The relation between a singular description like "the president of the U.S.A. in 1979" and the object to which it applies is a contingent relation: Descriptions are only contingently true of some unique individual. Descriptions do not give us certain knowledge of the existence of the individual that may in fact satisfy that description. Descriptions can be meaningful (i.e., sentences containing them are meaningful) even if there is no individual or more than one which satisfies that description. Singular descriptions when they *do* apply to some unique individual give us only indirect knowledge — "knowledge by description" — "about" the individual. We must turn now to consider how Russell's "knowledge by description" is connected with Descartes' *corrigible* knowledge.[38]

[36] Russell's Cartesian-derived distinction between knowledge by acquaintance and knowledge by description provides the setting for his theory of descriptions (Russell (1905)). It is developed more fully in relation to his "sense-data" theory (Russell (1912)), and later, in relation to the existence of objects (Russell (1914)), and finally, in relation to names and their bearers (Russell (1918)). As our concern, here, is with the epistemological presuppositions of Russell's theory of *reference*, I shall not be considering the sense data theory.

[37] Russell (1912), p. 119.

[38] Pears (1967) sums up Russell's epistemological distinction as follows: "The simplest way of presenting the contrast between these two kinds of knowledge is to say that you know the daughter of Hitler by description if you know that there is such a person, but have never come across her in your experience; and that you know her by acquaintance if you have come across her". (p. 72).

Russell's distinction between "knowledge by acquaintance" and "knowledge by description" is a distinction between different ways of knowing things. We have acquaintance with anything of which we are "immediately aware". "Immediately", here, means "without the intermediary of any process or information" (such as inferential processes or knowledge of truths). We know something by description if, *because* we are not acquainted with that thing, we know it only as the thing which uniquely possesses that property or set of properties given by the description. Knowledge by description means that we can know *about* some object without being acquainted with it. But we can know descriptions in cases where there is no real thing that possesses the properties described. Knowing the description of an object, therefore, can never guarantee that there is a real object. This is not so with acquaintance: If we possess knowledge by acquaintance, then it is knowledge of the real thing with which we are acquainted.[39] Acquaintance, in other words, carries the guarantee of access to the real. This "guarantee" consists in the incorrigibility of our knowledge of that with which we are acquainted. Russell's "knowledge by acquaintance" thus captures Descartes' notion of "privileged access". The "access", in the case of acquaintance, is to the real. This access is "privileged" because our knowledge of it is incorrigible. Conversely, knowledge by description fails to guarantee access to the real, for knowledge by description can never be a means to achieving acquaintance with an object. In fact, it is only things with which we are *not* acquainted that can be known by description. The *kind* of knowledge that descriptions give us is corrigible knowledge. Knowing the properties which some object might instantiate never ensures that there *is* a real object which instantiates them. Knowledge by description, therefore, opens up the possibility of error concerning what that knowledge is "about".

For Russell, the distinction between acquaintance and description is (a) a distinction between ways of knowing to which there corresponds (b) a distinction between things whose existence is known for certain, and things whose existence is not guaranteed. What links these two sets of distinctions is the incorrigibility which characterises knowledge by acquaintance. The existence of

---

[39] With the qualification: "sense-data theory aside".

things with which we are acquainted is guaranteed because knowledge of objects we are acquainted with is incorrigible knowledge.

Things with which we are not acquainted but know only by description are talked about by means of denoting phrase. Propositions that we use to talk about some thing which is known by description (i.e., propositions containing a denoting phase) do not contain that thing as a constituent.[40] A proposition which contains a genuine name, however, is a proposition about something with which we are acquainted — something whose existence is guaranteed. In such a case the object of our acquaintance occurs as a constituent of the propostion.

These epistemological considerations serve to show why Russell conflates "reference" with "occurring in a proposition" ("being a constituent of a proposition").[41] Russell's principle of atomicity[42] dictates that the meaning of a sentence (i.e., the proposition expressed by a sentence) is a function of the meaning of its constituents. Understanding a proposition involves knowing what the proposition is about. What the proposition is about is therefore a constituent of the proposition. If a sentence contains a genuine name as subject, then the sentence is about what is named. What is named is always something with which we are directly acquainted. Thus the proposition contains, as a constituent, that real individual with which we are acquainted.

The consequences of this where the notion of "meaning" is concerned are as follows:

Either (i) we can say that all expressions — both names and descriptions — have meaning. But then the meaning of a name is nothing other than its referent: Meaning = denotation. Taken this way, the meaning of an expression is the actual individual which is denoted — the individual which a sentence containing that expression as subject-term is about.

Or, (ii) we can make use of Mill's distinction between connotative and non-connotative terms, and say that only connotative terms have meaning: Meaning = connotation. This is to say that descriptions have meaning; names lack a meaning. Here, the meaning of a definite description cannot be the individual to

[40] Russell (1905), p. 119.
[41] *Ibid.*, see also Appendix A.
[42] Russell (1918); (1940).

which that description applies, for a description still has meaning (in this sense) in the absence of any existing individual which uniquely satisfies that description. To say that a singular description possesses meaning (whereas a name does not) is to say that a meaning can be assigned to any proposition in which that description occurs. This means, strictly speaking, that no singular description (Russell's "denoting phrase") has a meaning in isolation but that a truth-value can be assigned to any sentence in which that description occurs. It is the truth-value of the sentence which constitutes the meaning of the sentence. Here, meaning is assimilated to the truth-value of a sentence.[43]

On Russell's view, then, to talk about the meaning of an expression which occurs in a sentence is either (i) to talk about the reference of that expression, or (ii) to talk about the truth-conditions of the sentence which contains that expression. What these remarks demonstrate is that, where a two-levelled semantical framework is concerned, if we wish to retain a notion of "meaning",[44] then it must be assimilated to the level of reference.[45]

The identification of meaning with reference is anticipated in Russell's early work, *The Principles of Mathematics*, where he writes:

To have meaning, it seems to me, is a notion confusedly compounded of logical and psychological elements. *Words* all have meaning, in the simple sense that they are symbols which stand for something other than themselves. But a proposition, unless it happens to be linguistic, does not itself contain words: it contains the entities indicated by words. Thus meaning, in the sense in which words have meaning, is irrelevant to logic. But such concepts as *a man* have meaning in another sense: they are, so to speak, symbolic in their own logical nature, because they have the property which I call *denoting*. That is to say, when *a*

---

[43] Russell (1905), pp. 105; 116.

[44] On Russell's view, there is a sense in which we may dispense with "meaning" altogether. See Appendix A.

[45] If, following Frege, we take the reference of a sentence to be its truth-value, then the identification of meaning with a sentence's truth-value is to be understood as the assimilation of meaning to reference.

man occurs in a proposition (*e.g.* "I met a man in the street", the proposition is not about the concept *a man*, but about something quite different, some actual biped denoted by the concept. Thus concepts of this kind have meaning in a non-psychological sense. And in this sense, when we say "this is a man", we are making a proposition in which a concept is in some sense attached to what is not a concept. But when meaning is thus understood, the entity indicated by *John* does not have meaning, . . . ; and even among concepts, it is only those that denote that have meaning. The confusion is largely due, I believe, to the notion that *words* occur in propositions, which in turn is due to the notion that propositions are essentially mental and are to be identified with cognitions.[46]

For Russell, confusions concerning the meaning of expressions and the meaning of sentences containing those expressions are resolved if we appeal to the epistemological distinction of knowledge by acquaintance and knowledge by description. "In order to understand a proposition in which the name of a particular occurs, you must already be acquainted with that particular . . . to understand a symbol is to know what it stands for".[47] But not all propositions which are meaningful are ones about objects of acquaintance: ". . . when there is anything with which we do not have immediate acquaintance, but only definition by denoting phrases, then the propositions in which this thing is introduced by means of a denoting phrase do not really contain this thing as a constituent, but contain instead the constituents expressed by the several words of the denoting phrase".[48]

We can now see how Russell's epistemological theory sustains his theory of names and descriptions. First, names necessarily refer. This guarantee of reference is a *logical* feature of all and only names. A name logically cannot fail to pick out some particular existing individual. But the basis on which we ascribe this necessity to names is, for Russell, an *epistemological*

[46] Russell (1903), p. 47.
[47] Russell (1918), pp. 204—5.
[48] Russell (1905), p. 119.

one:[49] The individual which a name picks out cannot be something which is known to me by description, for the name by means of which I refer to that individual has no descriptive content.[50] The bearer of the name must, therefore, be something which I know by acquaintance and, therefore, something whose existence is known with certainty. The guarantee of reference which is a *logical* feature of names is a consequence of *epistemological* considerations, *viz.*, the incorrigibility which characterises my knowledge of the bearer of the name.

These considerations provide us with the conditions under which a given expression can be used as a name. But the doctrine of acquaintance goes further than this by telling us *which* expressions of our language *are* genuine names. The logical conclusion of the doctrine of acquaintance, where a theory of names is concerned, is Russell's theory of logically proper names. That is to say, having distinguished between the categories of names and descriptions on the basis of the semantic relation which characterises each, we can now, as the result of Russell's epistemological theory, state which expressions are to be assigned to the category of names.

It follows from Russell's epistemological theory that, if I possess knowledge by acquaintance, then (i) there must *be* some particular existing object with which I am acquainted, and (ii) this object must be present within my immediate sensory context.[51] Neither of these conditions obtains in the case of knowledge by description. That is to say, if I possess knowledge by description, then it does not follow that there exists some unique object which satisfies the description. Moreover, *what* I know is something which "we only reach by means of denoting phrases"[52] and is, therefore,

---

[49] The confusion of the logical with the psychological is particularly evident in Russell's lectures on "The Philosophy of Logical Atomism" (1918): "A name, in the narrow logical sense of a word whose meaning is a particular, can only be applied to a particular with which the speaker is acquainted, because you cannot name anything you are not acquainted with". (p. 201).

[50] In the sense that it is not *in virtue of* descriptive content that a name refers.

[51] This is required if our knowledge is to be incorrigible.

[52] Russell (1905), p. 103.

something which is absent from my immediate sensory context (otherwise it would be known to me by acquaintance rather than description). If it is only objects of acquaintance which can be picked out by names then the only expressions which are genuine names are those for which conditions (i) and (ii) obtain.[53] But these conditions are not, in general, satisfied by ordinary proper names such as "Winston Churchill" or "M. Mitterrand". We usually use these ordinary proper names to refer to individuals *in absentia*. The introduction of the Cartesian-derived requirement (ii) means that only those individuals which are demonstratively identified can be picked out by a name. For this reason Russell was led to conclude that the only genuine names are the demonstratives, "this" and "I".[54] He called these logically proper names.

The theory of names which results from Russell's two-levelled semantical framework can be summarised as follows: Names necessarily refer. That is to say, a genuine name cannot fail to pick out some particular existing object. The necessity, here, is a logical feature of names. It is a feature unique to names. Descriptions, on the other hand, may fail to pick out any existing individual or they may fail to pick out some unique individual. Where a description does apply to some individual, it is only a contingent matter that it does so.

There are, however, two reasons for dissatisfaction with Russell's theory of names as outlined here, and these both concern the intrusion of epistemological considerations into what is proposed

---

[53] "We say 'This is white'. If you agree that 'This is white', meaning the 'this' that you see, you are using 'this' as a proper name . . . . It is only when you use 'this' quite strictly, to stand for an actual object of sense, that it is really a proper name". (Russell (1918), p. 201). Russell adds that it is a peculiarity of such a term "that it seldom means the same thing two moments running and does not mean the same thing to the same speaker and to the hearer". (p. 201) – This is a logical consequence of insisting that it be only things within my immediate sensory context which can be picked out by a name.

[54] Although it seems that, for Russell, it is ultimately only the demonstrative "this" which is a genuine name: In "On the Nature of Acquaintance" (1914), Russell writes "The subject (of acquaintance) itself appears not to be acquainted with itself; but this does not prevent our theory from explaining the meaning of the word 'I' by the help of the meaning of the word 'this' . . . ." (p. 174).

as a logical theory. First, the distinction between the logical and the psychological is blurred. The necessity pertaining to names – which we express by saying that names *must* refer – is ultimately, for Russell, an epistemological necessity. Reference, the relation between a name and its bearer, is basically an epistemological relation: Reference is a function of our acquaintance with some object. The Cartesian-derived notion of acquaintance is a psychological notion. In Chapter V, we will examine in further detail the reasons why Russell's epistemological presuppositions can be called "psychological" and why, as a result of this, his theory of reference is said to be a psychologistic theory. A second related reason for objecting to Russell's theory of reference concerns his restrictions on the class of expressions which fall within the category of genuine names. If we wish to avoid a commitment to a Cartesian-based epistemology, we must be able to admit as genuine names expressions other than those whose referents are things which are known incorrigibly.

Post-Russellian philosophers such as Quine, Putnam and Kripke accept Russell's two-levelled semantical framework and, therefore, the theory that the guarantee of reference is a logical feature unique to names. However they claim to reject those epistemological presuppositions which, as we have seen, led Russell to the view that only certain demonstratives comprise the class of genuine names.[55] If Russell's account of reference is to be released from its epistemological setting then it must be dissociated from talk about "real objects with which we have direct acquaintance". There are two ways of doing this:

1. Reference, a semantic notion, can be defined syntactically in terms of grammatical position or role. Quine,[56] for example, treats reference in terms of the grammatical role or position of the singular term, "a" in the schema Fa. This position is subject to quantification: $(\exists x)\, Fx$. Referential position, then, means position accessible to the variables of quantification; referential role is the role of a bound variable in a sentence. Part of Quine's general thesis is that *all* singular terms (including ordinary proper names

---

[55] Prior (1971) shows critical acceptance of Russell's theory of names but, surprisingly, endorses his epistemological principles, claiming, ultimately, that it is only the demonstrative "I" which succeeds in genuinely naming.

[56] Quine (1960).

like "Socrates" as well as singular descriptions and demonstratives) can be eliminated by being confined to predicative position (the position of "*F*" in *Fa*). The referential work of the original singular term is now carried out by the variables of quantification. The value of such a variable is the individual to which we are onto-logically committed. Thus Russell's unsatisfactory notion of "real objects with which we are directly acquainted" is replaced here by the notion of "individuals to which we are ontologically com-mitted, these individuals being the values of the bound variables of quantification. At the same time however, Russell's theory of reference as a logical relation is retained: A genuine referring expression cannot fail to pick out some particular existing indi-vidudal.

2. Alternatively, we can retain the notion of reference as a semantical relation between a term and a real existing object. Kripke and Putnam who propose what has come to be called the "causal theory of names", defend the Russellian view of names as expressions which necessarily refer to some existing object, but the epistemological necessity which, for Russell, sustains the relation between a name and its bearer is, for these philosophers, replaced by a metaphysical necessity. Russell's account of reference in terms of a relation of acquaintance is re-expressed by the causal theorists as the thesis that names designate rigidly: To say that a name designates rigidly means that a name cannot fail to pick out some particular existing individual (and that it picks out that same individual in all possible worlds). The capacity of a name to designate rigidly is explained in terms of a causal connection between the demonstative introduction of an individual which is bestowed with a name, and subsequent uses of that name to pick out just that individual so "baptised". The necessity pertaining to names is thus a metaphysical rather than an epistemological necessity.

The views of Quine and those of the causal theorists will be submitted to closer scrutiny in later pages. Our present concern is to show that (a) the notion of reference which is explicated in terms of a two-levelled semantical framework is a plausible one – that the guarantee of reference which is accorded to names in terms of this framework can be seen as a logical feature, and (b) that the two-levelled framework provides us with an account of reference which is a genuine alternative to that which results from the Fregean three-levelled framework. It remains for us to show briefly how these two frameworks are incompatible with one another. But the degree of this incompatibility as well as its seriousness will only become evident when we see the consequences of each where a theory of intentionality is concerned.

§3. *Conclusion*

For Frege, the motivation for introducing the theory of sense and thereby the three-levelled semantical framework was a concern with the differing cognitive values of the two true identity statements, "$a = a$" and "$a = b$". In order to acknowledge this difference it is necessary to introduce, in addition to the reference of a sign, something else, *viz.*, the sense of a sign which is the mode in which the object referred to is presented. By doing so we can account for the fact that, in some contexts, different signs which have the same reference cannot be substituted for one another *salva veritate*.

For Russell, on the other hand, the motivation for introducing his theory of names as signs which necessarily refer and, thereby, the two-levelled semantical framework, was a concern about the existence or non-existence of those objects for which we use referring expressions. By restricting the class of names to those expressions for which there necessarily exists a referent (i.e. whose existence is guaranteed, in Russell's case, by our acquaintance with it), the problems surrounding expressions like "the present king of France" for which there exists no reference can be resolved. They are to be analysed as descriptions and thereby excluded from the category of names.

Our understanding of the notions "name" and "reference" will be radically different according to which semantical framework we choose to adopt. In terms of the Fregean framework, names necessarily have a sense although they need not refer to anything; in terms of the Russellian framework, names necessarily have a reference but they do not possess a sense. For Frege, reference is always a relation that is mediated by sense; for

Russell, the relation between a name and its bearer is direct or unmediated.[57]

We have already seen how Frege deals with the problem which pre-occupied Russell — that of referring expressions for which there exists no referent. For Frege, these expressions are names, but names are defined as signs which necessarily have a sense but which need not refer to anything. When words do not have their customary reference, for example when they occur in indirect speech, they refer to a sense. It remains now to show how Russell proposes to deal with the problem which led Frege to formulate his theory of sense — that of the differing cognitive values of the two true identity statements, "$a = a$" and "$a = b$".

Russell sets up the problem in the following way: George IV wished to know if Scott was the author of *Waverley* and, in fact, Scott *was* the author of *Waverley*. But it is not true that George IV wished to know if Scott was Scott.[58] This is an admission, on Russell's part, of the non-equivalence between the two true identity statements:

(1)   Scott is the author of *Waverley,* and
(2)   Scott is Scott.

As with Frege, the problem is to explain how an identity statement such as (1), which has the form of Frege's "$a = b$", can be informative as contrasted with (2), which is known *a priori.* Frege's explanation — that different signs (i.e., names) can refer to the same object because they have different senses — is not available to Russell. Russell's explanation invokes his distinction between names and descriptions: "When I say 'Scott is the author of *Waverley*' and that 'is' expresses identity, the reason why that

---

[57] Attempts to accommodate the notion of sense within a two-levelled semantical framework inevitably result in a distortion of *Frege's* notion of sense. In terms of such a framework, it is impossible for sense to be the *mediator* of reference. It cannot, therefore, be *Frege's* notion of sense which is exploited within such a framework. See Appendices A and B.

[58] Russell (1905). Russell's aim in this work is to show that, *contra* Frege, we do not have to appeal to the notion of meaning (i.e., sense) to account for failure of substitutivity in such contexts. In his later work — Russell (1918) pp. 244ff. — the aim is to show how failure of substitutivity here is to be explained by appeal to the distinction between names and descriptions.

identity can be asserted there truly and without tautology is just the fact that the one is a name and the other a description".[59]

It is because "Scott" in (2) occurs as a genuine name — i.e., it stands for something with which I am acquainted — that (2) is known *a priori*. The phrase, "the author of *Waverley*", in (1), does not stand for (i.e., name) anything: If it stood for something other than Scott, then (1) would be false; if it stood for (i.e., named) Scott, then (1) would be equivalent to (2).

A sentence containing the denoting phrase "the author of *Waverley*" as subject-term admits a "double denial".[60] That is to say, the sentence, "The author of *Waverley* is mortal" can be false either because there is no unique entity such that that entity wrote *Waverley*, or, if there *is* such an entity, because "is mortal" is falsely predicted of it. The phrase is, therefore, to be analysed as a description; descriptions are only contingently true or false of some individual; it is therefore informative to assert *of* some individual, that it satisfies the description.

A sentence containing the name "Scott" as subject-term does not admit a double denial: The sentence "Scott is mortal" (where "Scott" is a genuine name) can only be denied by saying "Scott is not mortal". We cannot deny the existence of something which is genuinely named. It is because "Scott" is a genuine name and "the author of *Waverley*" is a description that (1) can be informative, for (1) affirms that the predicate "wrote *Waverley*" is true of the individual named by "Scott".

But the theory of descriptions ensures that in analysing (1) as the informative sentence, "Scott wrote *Waverley*", we do not thereby cease to assert a true *identity* statement in (1). That is to say, the theory of descriptions by which we analyse *definite* descriptions allows us to retain the "is" of identity in (1), thereby marking off statements like (1) from ordinary predications such as

[59] Russell (1918) p. 247. Russell adds: "Or they might both be descriptions". It is not necessary for our purposes to consider assertions of identity between descriptions. For these do not provide the relevant contrast with identity statements of the form, "$a = a$". It is because in the *pair* of statements, "$a = a$" and "$a = b$", "a" occurs as a name and "b" as a description that the latter ("$a = b$") is a statement of the identity expressed by the former ("$a = a$").

[60] Russell (1918), p. 251.

"Scott is wise". Russell's analysis of the true identity statement expressed by (1) is as follows:

> The shortest statement of 'Scott is the author of *Waverley*' seems to be: 'Scott wrote *Waverley*; and it is always true of *y* that if *y* wrote *Waverley*, *y* is identical with Scott'. It is in this way that identity enters into 'Scott is the author of *Waverley*'; and it is owing to such uses that identity is worth affirming.[61]

For Russell, then, the difference between true identity statements of the form "$a = b$" and "$a = a$" is to be accounted for by appeal to the distinction between names and descriptions; for Frege it is to be explained by appeal to the notion of sense. One consequence of the Russellian approach to this problem concerns the analysis of sentences about the psychological.

The problem, as originally stated, was that of accounting for the difference between the true identity statements:

(1)   Scott is the author of *Waverley*, and
(2)   Scott is Scott,

where this difference is manifested in the non-equivalence of:

(3)   George IV wants to know if Scott is the author of *Waverley*, and
(4)   George IV wants to know if Scott is Scott.

For Russell, failure of substitutivity in (3) results from the fact that we cannot replace the *description*, "the author of *Waverley*" in (3), by the word "Scott" which is a *name* (in all its occurrences in (1) and (2)).

But if "Scott" in (3) is a name then we are committed to a particular way of interpreting (3). We cannot interpret (3) as:

(3')   George IV wants to know *whether* one person wrote *Waverley* and that man is Scott.

For, on this interpretation, "Scott" occurs predicatively: "is (called) Scott". Rather, we must interpret (3) as:

---

[61] Russell (1905), p. 118.

(3″)   George IV wants to know *of* Scott whether he wrote
          Waverley.[62]

The significance of this interpretation is that (3) is thereby analysed
not as a sentence which is solely about George IV, but as a sentence
about the two individuals, George IV and Scott. The words

"____ wants to know whether ____ wrote *Waverley*",

describe the relation that obtains between these two individuals.
We can abbreviate it as the predicate-letter, "R", and represent the
individuals George IV and Scott by the names "a" and "b",
respectively. We can thereby designate the relation by a sentence
of the form aRb. For Russell, all relations are "real" relations, that
is to say, they obtain between two existing individuals. This means
that any relational sentence will admit quantification:

$$aRb \longrightarrow (\exists x)\, xRb$$

$$aRb \longrightarrow (\exists x)\, aRx$$

Thus, for Russell, a sentence aRb means that a has the property of
R-ing-b, and also means that b has the property of being R'd-by-a.
Relational sentences can therefore be represented as predications:
Fx.

We can now represent (3″) as a sentence about Scott. The
sentence says, of the individual Scott, that he possesses the
property that George-IV-wants-to-know-of-him-whether-he-wrote-
Waverley. We can abbreviate this sentence as Fa, and we can admit
quantification so that the sentence implies something of the form:

(5) $(\exists x)\, Fx$.

(There exists something such that that thing has the property that
George-IV-wants-to-know-of-it-whether-it-wrote-*Waverley*).   But,
on this analysis, (3) turns out to be extensional for anything which
is identical with x in this formula will possess the property "F":

---

[62] In the case of a denoting phrase, the appropriate interpretation depends
upon whether the phrase has "primary" or "secondary" occurrence. "Any
statement in which a description has a primary occurrence implies that the
object described exists". Russell (1918), pp. 250–1. In short, when a denoting
phrase is used as a *name*, (has primary occurrence), the sentence containing
that phrase submits to the interpretation of (3″).

(6)   (x) (y) Fx & y = x $\longrightarrow$ Fy.

If "Frege's problem" concerning differences in cognitive values is approached in Russell's way — *via* a distinction between names and descriptions — then some sentences about the psychological can form extensional contexts. This cannot happen if we adhere to the Fregean framework. For Frege, *if* we wish to observe a difference between (3)˙ and (4), then we *must* appeal to the notion of sense. The words which tell us what George IV wants to know refer to a sense. The proposition expressed by those words (i.e., the sense that is referred to) cannot be analysed in such a way that the individual Scott (i.e., the customary reference of the word, "Scott") occurs in or is a constituent of that proposition.

Thus, for Frege, (3) must be analysed as an intensional construction — one which has the form of:

(7)   George IV wants to know if $(\exists x) x \phi$'s.

Here, the words "George-IV-want-to-know-if" are a function not of the individual Scott (or of any propostion in which the individual Scott occurs as a constituent), but rather as the function of a sense. This means that, if we abbreviate (3) as the propositional function $F(p)$, then we have a function which fails to satisfy Prior's extensional formula:

(8)   (p) (q): $p \equiv q . \supset . F(p) \equiv F(q)$.[63]

This does not mean that, for Frege, the law of identity expressed in (6) is violated. If (3) really *is* a sentence about the individual named by Scott then it would satisfy (6). But because, for Frege, if we are to observe the non-equivalence between (3) and (4) we *cannot* take the words which tell us what George IV wants to know as having their customary reference, we *cannot* analyse (3) as a sentence about the reference of the name "Scott". If failure of substitutivity in the case of sentences about the psychological is accounted for in the Fregean way, then those sentences must always be analysed as intensional functions.

[63] *Supra*, p. 34.

CHAPTER III

INTENTIONALITY, RELATIONS AND OBJECTS
I: THE RELATIONAL THEORY

§1. *Introduction*

Chisholm re-formulates Brentano's intentionality thesis in the following way:

> We may now re-express Brentano's thesis — or a thesis resembling that of Brentano — by reference to intentional sentences. Let us say (1) that we do not need to use intentional sentences when we describe non-psychological phenomena; we can express our beliefs about what is merely 'physical' in sentences which are not intentional. But (2) when we wish to describe perceiving, assuming, believing, knowing, wanting, hoping, and other such attitudes, then either (a) we must use sentences which are intentional or (b) we must use terms we do not need to use when we describe non-psychological phenomena.[1]

Intentional sentences, then, are to be contrasted with the sentences that we use to talk about non-psychological phenomena. There are two ways of understanding the expression, "sentences that we use to talk about non-psychological phenomena", *viz.*, "sentences about physical phenomena" and "sentences which are extensional". These indicate two different frameworks within which the problem of intentionality can be raised and discussed.

Chisholm's first criterion, *viz.*, absence of existential implication, tells us that intentional sentences are not like sentences such as "Jack kicks the stone", which designate a *physical* act. Sentences

[1] Chisholm (1957), pp. 172–3.

about any object-directed act — mental or physical — have the superficial grammatical form of a predicate expression with two referring terms: *Fab*. In the case of a physical act such as Jack's kicking the stone, there must exist some object, the stone, which is kicked. Thus if *Fab* represents a sentence about a physical act, the following holds true:

$$Fab \longrightarrow (\exists x)\, Fax.$$

That is to say, "Jack kicks the stone" implies "$(\exists x)\, x$ is kicked by Jack". This inference cannot be made where *Fab* represents a sentence about a psychological act such as Jack's thinking of a stone. We cannot infer from such a sentence that $(\exists x)\, x$ is thought of by Jack.

According to Chisholm's first criterion, then, intentional sentences are to be marked off from sentences which designate a physical activity. In this context, our understanding of intentionality will involve an appeal to a distinction between psychological and physical phenomena (i.e., acts).[2]

The second way of taking the expression, "sentences that we use to talk about non-psychological phenomena" is as follows: Sentences like "Tully is a Roman" lack intentionality. As we have already seen,[3] when such a sentence forms the *content* of someone's belief, thought, judgement, etc., as in "Tom believes that Tully is a Roman", then the sentence so formed is intentional by Chisholm's third criterion of non-substitutivity. Taken this way, intentionality is a feature of a certain class of sentences which are non-extensional. If intentionality is to be understood in this context, then we must appeal to the intensionality of language

---

[2] This distinction is not the same as Brentano's distinction between mental and physical phenomena (*cf. supra*, pp. 20–1): First, for the linguistic philosophers, the distinction between the two classes of phenomena (i.e., acts) is drawn on the basis of the "logical behaviour" of the sentences we use to talk about each, rather than on the basis of the modes in which phenomena are given. Second, the two distinctions need not be co-extensive. For those who follow Chisholm's thesis, perceiving — what Brentano calls "outer perception", and relegates to the domain of the physical — is included within the class of the psychological. The arguments for the intentionality of perception will be examined in Chapter IV.

[3] *Supra*, Chapter I.

and thereby invoke the distinction between extensional and non-extensional constructions.

In summary, we can say that there are two frameworks within which we can approach the intentionality thesis in its linguistic form. First we can appeal to a distinction between mental (i.e., psychological) phenomena and physical phenomena, where this distinction is expressed as the difference between the kinds of sentences we use to talk about each. The intentionality of a sentence which satisfies Chisholm's first criterion will be understood primarily in terms of this distinction. Second, we can appeal to the distinction between extensional and non-extensional constructions. The intentionality of a sentence which satisfies Chisholm's third criterion will be understood primarily in terms of this distinction.

The different frameworks provided by each set of distinctions suggest different starting points for approaching the topic of intentionality. These different frameworks, however, are not mutually exclusive or independent of one another.[4] For example, sentences we use to talk about *physical* phenomena will imply existence, and will also be *extensional* – i.e., will admit substitutivity. If Fred is the corporation manager then, from the sentence "Jack kicks Fred" we can infer "Jack kicks the corporation manager". But many of the puzzles surrounding intentionality arise from a complex interplay of these two frameworks. For example, in the case of psychological acts which do succeed in achieving objective reference, such as X's thinking of an existing Y, the object of thought is "real" in precisely the same way that the object of a physical act is "real": If I am thinking of Mrs. Thatcher, then the object of my thought is the same existing individual that I might also kick or strike. We can say in such a situation that a relation obtains between two existing individuals. But if this means that "objective reference" in the case of this act is to be characterised by appeal to Russell's relational sentences, discussed at the end of Chapter II, then we lose sight of the intentionality of the act, for the sentences which, on Russell's

---

[4] We have already seen one example of the interaction of these two frameworks in Chapter I, where it was shown that sentences about the psychological (primary those which give the content of thought) form a sub-class of sentences which are intensional.

account, are used to describe real relations are extensional. This way of understanding "objective reference" in the case of psychological acts which are directed to an existing object results in a denial of Chisholm's thesis which states that sentences about the psychological are irreducible to sentences that we use to talk about physical phenomena (i.e., extensional sentences).

The problem here concerns "objective reference" in the case of those psychological acts which are directed to some existing object. There are conflicting theories about what we are to understand by this notion. On the one hand, there is a case for saying that thinking about an existing object is radically different from thinking about a non-existing object, for the former constitutes a relation whereas the latter does not. (To assert that a relation does obtain in the case of the latter would, it seems, commit us to re-introducing Meinongian entities as the objects to which we are related). On the other hand, the thesis of intentionality dictates that the existence or non-existence of the object to which a psychological act is directed is irrelevant to the truth of a sentence about that act. Therefore, one would expect that existence or non-existence of the object is irrelevant to an analysis of such a sentence. Prior states the dilemma in the form of the triad:

(a) X's thinking of Y constitutes a relation between X and Y when Y exists, but (b) not when Y doesn't; but (c) X's thinking of Y is the same sort of thing whether Y exists or not. Something plainly has to be given up here; what will it be?[5]

"Relational theorists" accept (a) and (b) but reject (c); "Irreducibility theorists" accept (b) and (c) but reject (a).[6] "Relational theorists" are those who accept Russell's "real relation" as a

[5] Prior (1971), p. 130.

[6] The third alternative, that of accepting (a) and (c) but rejecting (b), would commit us to saying that all thinking constitutes a relation. This alternative is not available to us insofar as we are concerned with a theory of intentionality — i.e., with showing what is distinctive about the psychological. Godfrey-Smith (1979) points out that Prior's own resolution "was to say that ordinarily (c) is true and (a) is false. However he seems to have thought that in special circumstances, namely in the case of demonstrative reference, (a) is true, and the problems associated with (b) and (c) fail to arise". (p. 231).

paradigm of objective reference, and who attempt to force intentionality into this mould.[7] We will see, in this chapter, how this way of characterising objective reference results in the failure to account for the intentionality of some or, on a more extreme version, all psychological acts. The "irreducibility theorists" are those who reject the relational model and, like Chisholm, insist that intentionality is "what it is and not another thing". The puzzles that beset Anscombe's attempt to provide an account of the intentionality of sensation[8] exemplify the main difficulties for the irreducibility theory. These puzzles will be examined in Chapter IV. The problem with the irreducibility theory is that it fails to capture *both* the intentionality of the act *and* the fact of objective reference in the case of those psychological acts which are directed to an existing object.

The locus of our discussion in these two chapters is, then, the problem of objective reference in the case of those psychological acts which are directed to an existing object, such as X's thinking of an existing Y. On the relational theory which we turn to now, the problems arising for a theory of intentionality are traceable to the fact that the framework for our understanding of "objective reference" is quite explicitly a two-levelled one, based on Russell's theory of names.

§2. *Belief as a relation*

A natural way of interpreting Brentano's thesis of the object-directedness of the mental is to say that acts such as thinking, believing, judging, etc., constitute a relation between the subject and the object of the activity. For Brentano, the object of mental reference in the case of cognitive acts such as someone's judging that p (where p is some proposition) is not a proposition but the object that the proposition is about. Thus, if A judges that a unicorn does not exist, the object to which A is intentionally

---

[7] The "relational theory" of objects of thought which is a logical consequence of Russell's theory of names and of relations is developed explicitly in Prior (1971).

[8] Anscombe (1965).

related is a unicorn and not a unicorn's non-existence.[9] On this interpretation of Brentano's thesis then we could say that sentences about judging, believing, thinking, etc., have the form of a predicate function taking two names as arguments:

_____ believes _____

Russell's early attempts to construe belief as a relation is consistent with such an interpretation but this, it seems, is where the similarity ends. For Brentano, the objects to which we are related when we believe or judge something are intentionally in-existent. For Russell, on the other hand, the only objects to which we can stand in a (genuine) relation are existing things.

The problem of non-existing objects of thought is one which arises for sentences which are demonstrably about *objects* of thought, that is to say, sentences with a direct object such as "*X* thinks of *Y*", which have the logical form of a two-place predicate. If we are to treat believing, judging, etc., as relations we must be able to say what it is that the believer, judger, etc., is related to; and this means that we must have some theory about the way in which sentences telling us *what* is believed or judged (such as "*A* believes *p*") are to be analysed as sentences telling us what the belief or judgement is *about*.

In this task, we must begin by recalling a distinction made earlier,[10] concerning "objects" of thought, *viz.*, the distinction between *what* we think (the *content* of thought), on the one hand, and what we think *about* (the *object* of thought), on the other. Sentences containing a "that-" clause, e.g., *A* believes that *p*, exemplify the first; sentences of direct-object form, e.g., *A* thinks of *Y*, exemplify the second. *What* we think may be true or false; what we think *about* may be non-existent. The relational theory is applicable primarily to objects of thought. As Prior states it: "*X*'s thinking of *Y* constitutes a relation between *X* and *Y* when *Y* exists, but . . . not when *Y* doesn't". Sentences containing a "that-" clause pose a two-fold problem for the relational theorist. First, if *A*'s thinking (or believing, judging, etc.,) *that p* can constitute a relation, what is it that *A* is related *to*? A fact? A

[9] *Supra*, p. 32n.
[10] *Supra*, pp. 32ff.

proposition? Or the constituents into which the proposition can be analysed? Second, our analysis of the thinking, believing, etc., here, in the form of a relation must be an analysis which is consistent with our saying that *what* is thought, believed, etc., can be *false*. These problems relating to *what* we think are central to Russell's attempts to construe belief as a relation. After we have examined these problems we will turn, in §3, to an alternative approach that is available to the relational theorist *viz.*, an approach which begins with a consideration of what we think *about*. We can then see the consequences of this approach for those sentences giving *what* we think.

If *A* believes some proposition *p*, what is it that *A* is related to? This question is the source of those problems surrounding Russell's attempts to construe belief as a relation. Russell presents us with two different theories in the attempt to provide a relational account of belief. He points out first that belief, unlike knowledge, can be true or false.[11] Second, the truth or falsity of a belief depends not on the belief but on something outside that belief: ". . . although truth and falsehood are properties of beliefs, they are properties dependent upon the relations of the beliefs to other things, not upon any internal quality of the beliefs".[12] The first of these observations, concerning the difference between knowledge (or perception) and belief, provides the setting for Russell's "multiple relation" theory of belief;[13] the second, concerning the difference between true and false beliefs, provides the setting for his theory of "beliefs as pointers to facts".[14]

The second of these − the theory of "beliefs as pointers to facts" − concerns the relation between what is believed and the fact that makes that belief true or false. It is developed in the course of his attempt to dispense with propositions as entities which exist in addition to facts. There are true and false propositions, but not true and false facts. Dispensing with propositions creates problems concerning the status of objects of belief. For

[11] Russell (1912), p. 119.

[12] *Ibid.*, p. 121.

[13] *Ibid.*; also, Russell (1918) pp. 218ff. The labels of each of these theories are suggested by Prior (1971), pp. 7, 10.

[14] Russell (1921) pp. 271−3. Also Russell (1918), p. 223.

> You cannot say that you believe *facts*, because your beliefs are sometimes wrong . . . . Wherever it is facts alone that are involved, error is impossible . . .[15]

But the difficulty of saying that you believe *propositions* is that "propositions are nothing".[16] We cannot say that "in addition to facts there are also these curious shadowy things going about such as 'That today is Wednesday' when in fact it is Tuesday".[17] Russell's problem is to account for the fact that beliefs can be true or false without thereby saying that belief is a relation between the believer and some proposition. Russell's proposed solution is as follows:

> If today is not Tuesday, this fact is the objective of your belief that today is Tuesday. But obviously the relation of your belief to the fact is different in this case from what it is in the case when today is Tuesday. We may say, metaphorically, that when today is Tuesday, your belief that it is Tuesday points *towards* the fact, whereas, when today is not Tuesday, your belief points *away from* the fact . . . If, on Tuesday, one man believes that it is Tuesday while another believes that it is not Tuesday, their beliefs have the same objective, namely the fact that it is Tuesday, but the true belief points towards the fact while the false one points away from it.[18]

People holding contradictory beliefs (e.g., *A*'s believing that snow is white and *B*'s believing that snow is not white) are, then, related to the same fact, but they are, somehow, related in different ways. As Prior points out, this theory "either gives no account at all of *what is believed*, or else makes this something different when the belief is false and when it is true".[19] Prior illustrates this with the example:

> When I believe . . . that Jones is musical, what I believe is the fact that Jones is musical, if that *is* a fact; but if it is not a fact,

[15] Russell (1918), pp. 222–3.
[16] *Ibid.*, p. 223.
[17] *Ibid.*
[18] Russell (1921), p. 272.
[19] Prior (1971), p. 10.

what I believe, when I believe that Jones is musical, is the fact that Jones is *not* musical, only I somehow don't believe this the right way.[20]

Elsewhere Russell states that, although it is sometimes "linguistically convenient"[21] to talk as if belief were a two-termed relation between a believer and some single object believed, in general,

> It is not accurate to say 'I believe the proposition *p*' and regard the occurrence as a twofold relation between me and *p*. The logical form is just the same whether you believe a false or a true proposition . . . . The belief does not really contain a proposition as a constituent but only the constituents of the proposition as constituents.[22]

Given that there are no propositions, belief cannot consist in a two-termed relation between the believer and a single object, *viz.*, a propositon; it is, rather, a relation to those constituents into which a proposition is analysed. If belief were to be understood in this way as a many-termed relation, then, as Russell saw it, we could provide a satisfactory analysis of false belief (i.e., the believing of a false proposition). For "a false proposition, must, wherever it occurs, be subject to analyses, be taken to pieces, pulled to bits, and shown to be simply separate pieces of one fact in which the false proposition has been analysed away".[23] In this version of the multiple relation theory of belief, Russell's rejection of the dyadic-relation theory consists in the following claim: There are false beliefs; if belief consisted in a two-termed relation, we would have to say in the case of a false belief that what the believer is related to is a proposition. For Russell there are no propositions.

On an earlier version of the multiple relation theory the arguments against the dyadic-relation theory of belief take a different form.[24] Russell's concern, here, is to distinguish belief from

---

[20] *Ibid.*
[21] Russell (1918), p. 224.
[22] *Ibid.*
[23] *Ibid.*, pp. 223–4.
[24] Russell (1912), pp. 119ff.

knowledge which is a two-termed relation between the knower and the fact known. Russell argues here that if belief were a two-termed relation between the believer and a single object, then there would be no such thing as false belief:

> Othello believes falsely that Desdemona loves Cassio. We cannot say that this belief consists in a relation to a single object, 'Desdemona's love for Cassio', for, if there were such an object, the belief would be true. There is, in fact, no such object, and, therefore Othello cannot have any relation to such an object. Hence his belief cannot possibly consist in a relation to this object.[25]

The rejection of the dyadic-relation theory, here, consists in the following: If belief consisted in a relation of the believer to a single object, then all beliefs would be true beliefs.

Russell proposes, against the dyadic-relation theory of belief, that A's believing p be understood as a many-termed relation between the believer and the various constituents of the proposition believed. In the early version of this theory, Othello's believing that Desdemona loves Cassio is to be seen as a relation (*viz.*, that of believing) which obtains between Othello and Desdemona and loving and Cassio:

> Desdemona and loving and Cassio must all be terms in the relation which subsists when Othello believes that Desdemona loves Cassio. This relation, therefore, is a relation of four terms, since Othello also is one of the terms of the relation.[26]

When the various elements, Desdemona and loving and Cassio, are in fact "knit together"[27] in a complex which corresponds to the belief (i.e., in the same order as they are believed), then the belief is true; where there is no such complex formed by the various constituents in that order, then the belief is false. The notion of a fact as a complex in which certain elements are "knit together" in

[25] *Ibid.*, p. 124.
[26] *Ibid.*, p. 125.
[27] *Ibid.*, p. 126.

a certain order, is left unexplained by Russell; similarly, we are left without any account of how such a complex might succeed or fail in corresponding to a belief. But, from the point of view of Russell's own theory of relations, a main difficulty with this version of the multiple relation theory of belief is that it introduces, as objects to which we can be related, abstract entities corresponding to words such as "loving" in addition to objects such as those corresponding to the words "Desdemona" and "Cassio". On this version of the multiple relation theory of belief, the four-termed relation of believing can be expressed as a predicate function,

(1) ＿＿ believes ＿＿＿, ＿＿＿, ＿＿＿,

but the arguments of the function will include names of abstract entities such as loving.

Because, for Russell, it is only existing things to which one can be related, and because existing things are those things which are possible objects of acquaintance, we cannot say that a relation can obtain between a believer and an entity such as "loving" (or "x's love"). In his later version of the multiple relation theory,[28] Russell says:

> ... every theory of error sooner or later wrecks itself by assuming the existence of the non-existent. As when I say 'Desdemona loves Cassio', it seems as if you have a non-existent love between Desdemona and Cassio, but that is just as wrong as a non-existent unicorn ... .[29]

To avoid "assuming the existence of the non-existent", *viz.*, an "entity" named by the noun "loving", Russell insists in this later version of the theory that the word "loves" continue to function

---

[28] Russell (1918), pp. 224ff.

[29] *Ibid.*, p. 225. This statement is ambiguous. Is the existence of loving not to be assumed because it is *false* that Desdemona loves Cassio? Or because loving is an *abstract* entity? The context of the statement suggests the latter interpretation, for we are enjoined to treat "loves" as a verb not as a noun, so that no abstract entities need be introduced. Moreover, on the earlier version of this theory, it is not *Desdemona's* (non-existent) love which is a constituent of what is believed but, rather, the entity, loving, *per se*.

as a verb and not as a substantive. So, on this version, Othello's believing that Desdemona loves Cassio would still constitute a many-termed relation between Othello and the constituents of his belief, but this time the relation would be a complex one obtaining between Othello and Desdemona and Cassio. In the particular example we are using, this relation would be expressed as a predicate function, something like:

(2) ____ believes ____ to love ____ ,

which takes only names of concrete individuals as arguments. But the difficulty with this theory is that it requires us to provide different accounts of the relation of believing depending on what it is that is believed in each case. For example, our account of believing in (2) above will be different from the account we give of the relation expressed by:

(2′) ____ believes ____ to hate ____ ,

for the relations in (2) and (2′) have nothing in common. Russell seems to have been aware of this consequence for he says "belief itself cannot be treated as being a proper sort of single term. Belief will really have to have different logical forms according to the nature of what is believed".[30] Russell's recognition of this, in fact, signals the abandonment of the attempt to force "believing" into the mould of a relation. We will see later in this chapter what kind of account is proposed to replace it.

On any version of a relational theory of believing (or thinking, etc.) there will be difficulties surrounding the analysis of beliefs which are not about any particular individual. If Othello believes there is someone who is unfaithful, in the sense that it is true *of someone* that Othello believes *she* (or *he*) is unfaithful, then (if we are unmoved by any of the above objections), we might accept a relational theory of Othello's belief. But if Othello's belief is that someone, i.e., not anyone in particular − just someone, is unfaithful, it would seem impossible to cast this belief in the form of a many-termed relation. Similar problems arise in the case of Othello's believing that nobody is unfaithful, for here it would seem that there is no relation at all, for there is nothing to which Othello stands related. And yet, it seems, we would want to

---

[30] *Ibid.*, p. 226.

distinguish between Othello's not believing anything and Othello's believing that no-one is unfaithful.

The difficulties here arise from the fact that on the relational theory it is presupposed that all cases of "believing *that*" are disguised cases of "thinking *of* (or *about*)". If this presupposition were true, there would be a case for seriously pursuing a relational theory of belief. However, on the basis of the examples given, it would seem that, at least sometimes, there is a logical difference between cases of "believing of" and cases of "believing that". But the latter cannot even be expressed in terms of the relational approach to belief discussed here.

§3. *"Objects" of thought*

The kinds of difficulties that we have seen to arise in the course of Russell's attempts to construe belief as a relation are those associated with the question, What is it that we are related to in the case of believing? But we can attempt a relation-based account of the psychological from a different starting-point. Instead of asking of any particular psychological act, such as thinking, believing, judging, etc., what it is that we are related to, we can begin with a consideration of the kinds of things to which we *can* stand in a genuine relation (as the relational theorist sees it) when we think or believe something about them. If we can state the conditions under which something can constitute a genuine "object" of thought in this sense, we will be able to determine the conditions under which cognitive acts such as thinking, believing, etc., constitute a real relation.

We have already seen how, for Russell, if a sentence contains a genuine name as subject, then the sentence is *about* the particular existing individual that is the bearer of that name. The individual is a constituent of the meaning of the sentence. In this strict sense of "about", it is only particular existing individuals that sentences can be "about". The attempt to force intentionality into the mould of a real relation represents this same strict interpretation of "about" in the case of "what can be thought *about*". Russell interprets this phrase in such a way that only those things which *exist* − i.e., are "real" − can be thought *about*. Thus only real, existing things can be "objects" of thought. The existence of a thing is, for Russell, a necessary but not a sufficient condition for that thing's being an object of thought. As we shall see later, there is an epistemological restriction on the kinds of existing things that can be objects of thought — only what is *infallibly known* to exist can be an object of thought, for Russell. If Y is a genuine object of thought in A's thinking of Y, then a sentence describing A's thinking designates a real relation between A and Y. Thus the sentence, "A thinks of Y" admits quantification: $(\exists x)$ x is thought of by A. All genuine cases of thinking about are expressed in sentences which admit quantification in this way.

A's thinking about a non-existing Z — for example, Tom's thinking about Pegasus — is therefore not really a thinking "about" anything. The sentence, "A thinks of Z" (when Z does not exist), does not designate a relation for there is no object to which A is related, here. Thus not all cases of thinking *of* are genuine cases of thinking *about*: Only existing things can be thought *about*; only existing things can be *objects* of thought, for Russell. What kind of analysis, then, are we to give of a sentence, "A thinks of Z", when Z does not exist?

A's thinking of Z here might be a case of thinking *that* Z exists. In this case we would describe A's thinking in a sentence of the form, "A thinks that $(\exists x)$ x is Z". Tom's thinking of Pegasus would thus be analysed as "Tom thinks that there is something such that it is Pegasus".[31] But not all cases of thinking which are directed to something non-existent are cases of thinking *that* that thing *exists*. If A's thinking of Z, in the present example, is not a case of A's thinking *that Z exists,* it must still, nonetheless, be a case of thinking *that*, and not a case of thinking *of*. Therefore, it must be a case of A's thinking that Z ϕ's. In this case the same mode of analysis is applicable. A's thinking *something* of a non-existing Z must be analyzed as "A thinks that $(\exists x)$ x is Z and x ϕ's". On this analysis, Tom's thinking of Pegasus would be rendered as "Tom thinks that there is something such that it is Pegasus and it ϕ's". Thus all cases of (what we informally call) "thinking of" which are not genuine cases of thinking *about* (in

---

[31] This analysis shows, of course, that "Pegasus" is not a genuine name but a "sort of truncated or telescoped description . . . ." Russell (1918), p. 243.

Russell's sense) are really cases of thinking *that*. The difference between the two is a difference in the quantificational scope of each kind of sentence when analysed: Genuine cases of thinking *about* are described in sentences which are analysable into the form of

$(\exists x)$ x is thought of by . . .

Cases of thinking *that* which are not genuine cases of thinking about are described in sentences which are analysable into the form of

. . . thinks that $(\exists x)$ x . . .

Sentences which have the form of ". . . thinks that" followed by a proposition are, as we saw earlier, sentences about the *content* of someone's thought.[32] Non-existent things which are thought of must therefore be characterised in terms of the content of someone's thought. The content of someone's thought is always a proposition. Thus, if thinking of a non-existent Z is not a case of thinking that there exists something which is a Z, then it must be a case of thinking *something* of Z — that is, a case of thinking that $Z \phi$'s. So if my thinking "of" Pegasus is not a case of simply thinking that Pegasus exists, it must be a case of thinking that there exists something which is Pegasus and which ϕ's. The content of my thought cannot be "Pegasus". It must be some proposition.

Thus, on the relational view, all cases of thinking *of* which are genuine cases of thinking *about* constitute real relations. Cases such as thinking of a non-existent Z are not really cases of thinking *about* at all. Talk about A's thinking of a non-existent Z is really talk about the *content* of A's thinking, and can never be regarded as talk about the *object* of thought. Implied here is the view that talk about the content of someone's thought can never be a means to talking about the object of someone's thought. Sentences we use to talk about the *content* of someone's thought have the form of: A thinks that $(\exists x)$ x is . . .; sentences we use to talk about the *object* of someone's thought have the form of: $(\exists x)$ x is thought by . . . to . . . (or is thought of by . . .). No inference can be made from sentences of the first form to sentences of the second form.

[32] *Supra*, Ch. 1. To describe the proposition following the "that-" clause as the "*content*" of someone's thought is a non-Russellian characterisation.

On this analysis, what account can be given of the relation between the content and the object of someone's thought when, for instance, *A* thinks *that* (an existing) *Y* is ϕ? To ask this is to ask: Under what conditions can a cognitive activity (a thinking-*that*) constitute a real relation (i.e., an instance of thinking *about*)? That is to say, what are the conditions for asserting a formal equivalence between the following:

(1) *A* thinks that *Y* is ϕ

(2) *A* thinks of *Y* that it is ϕ

The existence of some individual, *Y*, is a necessary but not a sufficient condition for securing this equivalence. It may be true that I think *of* some individual, *viz.*, Tully, that he is a Roman (as in 2); but it may, at the same time, be false that I think *that* Tully is a Roman (as in 1). For the individual to which I am related in 2 may be known to me only as Cicero. Similarly, I may think *that* someone is in the next room. If there is someone in the next room, then it is not necessarily true that it is *that* person of whom I think that *he* is in the next room.

A further restriction, then, is needed on the assumption that only what really exists can be thought of. To understand the nature of this restriction it is helpful to talk about "saying of" instead of "thinking of" (at the same time retaining the distinction between ϕing *of* and ϕing *that*). Thus cases of "saying of" are to be expressed as "$(\exists x) \, x$ is said by . . . to . . ."; "saying that" expressed as ". . . says that $(\exists x) \, x$ . . ."). If the following is to constitute a real relation:

(1') *A* says that *Y* is ϕ,

then it must be equivalent to

(2') *A* says of *Y* that it is ϕ.

This equivalence only obtains if the individual *Y*, in 1' is referred to by a genuine name. If *A* uses a genuine name to refer to some individual *Y*, then the individual *Y* is known to *A* by direct acquaintance. Thus the equivalence between 1' and 2', which is the condition under which a cognitive activity constitutes a real relation, is secured in virtue of the epistemological principle of direct acquaintance. Thus, for Russell (and also for Prior) the epistemological doctrine of knowledge by acquaintance is what secures the connection between the content and object of thought.

When A's saying (or thinking or believing, etc.) *that Y ϕ's* constitutes a real relation (that of A's saying *of Y* that it ϕ's) then the sentence we use to talk about it is extensional. It follows from the relational account so far given, that there are some "psychological phenomena", *viz.*, thinking of an existing Y, which can be talked about in sentences that are not intentional – i.e., sentences that are extensional. This conflicts with Chisholm's statement that, when we talk about the psychological, we must use sentences which are intentional.

The radical nature of this conflict becomes evident when we see that Russell's claim consists in saying that, in talking about some psychological phenomena, we *must* use sentences that are extensional. This is particularly clear when we look at the consequence of Russell's theory where perception is concerned.[33] Perception is a paradigm case of an intentional activity which achieves "objective reference". For "perceives", in its most common use, is taken to mean a psychological activity which necessitates that there exist some object. On the relational theory perceiving always constitutes a real relation between the perceiving subject and the object perceived. Therefore, on the relational view, any sentence about perceiving will necessarily be extensional.

The specific problem, here, concerns the "transparency" of perception. To assert that perceiving necessitates that there exist some object is to assert that perception is transparent. The kind of transparency that is ascribed to perception by Russell and his followers I shall call "logical transparency". To say that "perceives" is logically transparent is to say that any sentence containing the verb "perceives" (i) admits quantification and (ii) admits substitutivity. Any sentence containing "perceives" will fail to satisfy Chisholm's first and third criteria.

Commitment to Russell's notion of a "real" relation and the associated notion of "real, existing individual" is not a necessary

---

[33] Here, again, we must distance the account of perception which follows, logically from Russell's theory of names and of relations from his "sense-data" theory of perception.

part of accepting the view that perception ("perceives") is "logically transparent". Quine,[34] for example, captures the logical transparency of perception in his doctrine of "*referentially* transparent contexts". In the sentence, "*A* perceives *o*", "*A* perceives . . ." forms a referentially transparent context if it can be quantified into and, therefore, admits substitutivity. Such contexts are, then, extensional. However, in Quine's case, there is no appeal to "real relations" and "real" existing things. The context "*A* perceives . . ." is referentially transparent, if the singular term, "*o*" which occurs in that context occupies purely referential position. "Purely referential position" is the position that is subject to quantification: it is the position occupied by a variable that is bound by the quantifier which stands outside of the context: "$(\exists x) A$ perceives x".

One consequence of the Russell-Quine approach is the *reduction* of the intentional to the extensional: We can say all we want to say about psychological phenomena in sentences which are *extensional*. We have seen how this is so when, for Russell, the psychological act constitutes a real relation or, for Quine, when the phenomenon is talked about in a sentence which is referentially transparent. However the reductivist claim requires that we show how those recalcitrant cases of thinking of a *non-existent Z* or believing *that* . . . might also be talked about in sentences which are extensional. We have already seen how, for Russell, *A*'s thinking of a non-existent *Z* is simply a disguised case of *A*'s thinking *that* . . . . A sentence about *A*'s thinking *that* something is the case is a sentence about *A*. It is a sentence which ascribes to *A* the property of thinking-a-certain-proposition, *p*. "Thinking (or believing) *p*" is now predicated of "*A*". In this predication, "*p*" occurs non-transparently (to borrow from Russell's earlier terminology). It does not occur as a constituent of the sentence "*A* believes *p*". Russell suggests that to say that "*A* believes *p*" is to say that "he is in one of a number of describable states" and, further, that this "psychological" state can in fact be described in purely physical terms.[35] Quine develops this suggestion by attempting to show that descriptions of "psychological states"

[34] Quine (1960), pp. 141ff.
[35] Russell (1940), pp. 267ff.

can be reduced to descriptions of behaviour: To say that A is in one of a number of describable "psychological" states is to say nothing more than that A is disposed to respond behaviourally in certain ways to certain stimuli under certain conditions.[36] So-called "psychological phenomena" are nothing other then dispositions to behave in certain ways; behavioural dispositions are describable in sentences which are extensional; therefore the intentional can be eliminated altogether.

There are two moves in this general development of Russell's original insights. These two moves represent (i) extensionalism — the claim that the intentional can be reduced to the extensional; and, (ii) behaviourism — the claim that the intentional can be eliminated altogether. The first of these states that we can say all we want to say about psychological phenomena in sentences which are extensional; the second states that the "psychological" is, in fact, nothing other than physical states of affairs.

These consequences of Russell's attempt to accommodate intentionality into his theory of relations are in direct conflict with Chisholm's thesis of intentionality. For Chisholm: (i) in talking about the psychological we *must* use sentences which are intentional (i.e., non-extensional); (ii) sentences about psychological phenomena cannot be translated into sentences about physical (i.e., nonpsychological) phenomena.

§4. *Conclusion*

We have seen here two different ways of attempting to characterise objects of thought in terms of the relational theory. The first, consistent with Brentano's thesis of the object-directedness of the mental, begins with the assumption that all sentences about the psychological have the logical form of a relational sentence, that is, a predicate function taking names as arguments. The second approach is premissed on Russell's own theory of relations which tells us that only those things which (are infallibly known to) exist can be genuine objects of a relation, and it is *only* when this condition is satisfied that a cognitive act such as thinking, believing, etc., can be analysed in terms of a relational sentence.

---

[36] Quine (1960)

The difficulties surrounding Russell's attempts to construct a relational theory of belief are those arising from the question, What is it that the believer is related to in the case of A's believing p? We cannot say it is a fact, for then there would be no such thing as false belief; but if, to allow for the possibility of false belief, we say that it is a proposition, then we must admit that such entities as false propositions exist in addition to facts (which, we might say, are true propositions); if we propose that the believer is related to the constituents into which the proposition can be analysed, then we must either admit the existence of abstract entities such as loving or fidelity, or else we must resign ourselves to the fact that there is nothing common to different instances of believing.

But there are difficulties of a more general kind with any attempt to construe belief as a relation. From A's believing p & q, we are entitled to infer that A believes p. But, if "believes" is a two-place predicate taking names as arguments, as a relational theory requires, then this inference is blocked, for "p & q" and "p" are different names. A relational theory of belief, therefore, obscures the internal logical structure of the "content" of a belief (i.e., the proposition believed). This does not happen if we treat the verb "believes" as part of an operator which forms a sentence from another sentence – the kind of analysis which we have seen to be appropriate in treating "believes", etc., as intensional functions.[37] Moreover, if all cases of believing are to be analysed as relations in this way, then no sentences about believing will satisfy the criteria of absence of existential implication or of non-substitutivity. For if all sentences about believing *do* have the logical form of a predicate function taking names as arguments, then, according to Russell's account of relational sentences,[38] those sentences will imply existence and admit substitutivity. "Believes", on this account, will always be an extensional function, *viz.*, one which satisfies the formula:

$$(p)\,(q)\colon p \equiv q \,.\, \supset \,.\, F(p) \equiv F(q)^{39}$$

[37] *Supra*, Chapter I §4.

[38] *Supra*, Chapter II §3.

[39] *Supra*, p. 34. On this analysis, "A believes p" fails to satisfy Chisholm's second criteria – non-implication of truth or falsity – as well as the other two. For here, "A believes" is a truth-function of "p": The value of the function $F(p)$ depends upon the truth of p. Chisholm's second criterion tells us that "A believes" is not a truth-function of "p".

On the second approach, there is no presumption that all psychological acts constitute a relation and, consequently, no problems about trying to say what it is that the subject of such acts is related *to*. On this approach, the relational theorist begins with the premise that the subject can *only* be related to things which (are infallibly known to) exist. On this approach, the only cases where believing, thinking, etc., constitute relations are those in which this condition is satisfied. Here, it is only those cases of believing, thinking, etc., which *are* genuine relations that are described in relational sentences – i.e., sentences which imply existence and admit substitutivity and which are, therefore, extensional sentences. However it is a logical consequence of this theory, as we have seen, that cases of thinking, believing, etc., which do not constitute genuine relations and are, therefore, not described in relational sentences are nonetheless described in sentences which are extensional. For, if a sentence describing *A*'s believing *p* is not a relational sentence it is, nonetheless, a sentence *about* some existing individual *A* and, for this reason, is extensional.

The first of these approaches, exemplified by Russell's theory of belief as a relation, commits us to the view that all sentences about believing are relational sentences and, therefore, sentences which fail to satisfy the criteria for intentionality; the second approach, although it allows that only some sentences about believing, may be relational sentences, nonetheless leads to the view that all sentences about believing are extensional.

The relational theory *per se*, as well as the consequences of this theory, are in direct conflict with a theory of intentionality. A theory of intentionality must incorporate the thesis that mental phenomena can succeed in achieving objective reference. If we accept a moderate version of the relational theory, which admits that only *some* sentences about the psychological – *viz.*, those which are relational – are non-intentional, then we remove from the class of the intentional precisely those sentences about acts which *do* succeed in achieving objective reference (e.g., thinking of an existing *Y*). It is just these sentences (about "successful" acts of mental reference) which the revised intentionality thesis was designed to include. If we accept the more extreme extensionalist and behaviourist consequences of the relational theory, then we dismiss the intentional altogether.

CHAPTER IV

INTENTIONALITY, RELATIONS AND OBJECTS
II: THE IRREDUCIBILITY THEORY

§1. *Introduction*

An alternative approach to the problem of how individual acts are capable of objective reference is that offered by philosophers who claim that intentionality is irreducible — that intentionality is "what it is and not another thing". All thought is intentional. The intentionality of thought cannot be reduced to anything else, nor can it be eliminated altogether. Thus the irreducibility theory is opposed to the relational theory that we have been discussing, for it denies *both* that intentional sentences can be reduced to extensional constructions, *and* the possible consequence of this view, that the intentional can be eliminated altogether. After a brief discussion of Chisholm's own arguments for the thesis that intentionality is irreducible, I shall turn to some of the problems that arise for such a thesis — *viz.*, those problems which beset Anscombe's attempts to provide an account of the intentionality of sensation.

For Chisholm, talk about the psychological is characterised by intentionality. The criteria for a sentence's being intentional are linguistic criteria, as we have seen. An important corollary of this thesis is that talk about non-psychological phenomena must be non-intentional. That is to say, in talking about the non-psychological, we must use sentences which do not satisfy the criteria given. Expressed in this way, the thesis of intentionality stands opposed to certain kinds of behaviourism and physicalism which seek to eliminate the psychological in favour of non-psychological or "purely physical" phenomena. As Chisholm sees it, the failure of such theories is demonstrated by the fact that intentional constructions defy translation into non-intentional constructions.

For example, Chisholm[1] seeks to show that behaviourist renderings of psychological attitudes fail, because ultimately we must still have recourse to intentional language to talk about these "de-psychologised" phenomena, or else we must recognise a covert psychological aspect to the substitute phenomena. To re-express the psychological attitude of A's thinking of x in terms of linguistic behaviour such as A's disposition to utter a sentence which *designates* or *refers* to x requires that we use intentional language to describe that behaviour. For, according to Chisholm, the terms "designate" and "refer" are intentional in virtue of the first criterion (lack of existential implication).

Chisholm's notion of "referring", here, is clearly opposed to that of Russell. For Russell, if some expression refers to x, then necessarily there exists some object, x. And if some language-user A uses an expression N to refer to x, then necessarily there exists some object, x, to which A is related. For Chisholm, however, this is not so. If an expression, N, refers to something, it does not follow either that that thing exists or that it does not exist. Chisholm explains his position as follows:

> When we talk about what is 'designated' or 'referred to' by words or sentences, our own sentences are intentional. When we affirm the sentence 'In German, *Einhorn* designates, or refers to, unicorns', we do not imply that there are any unicorns and we do not imply that there are not; and similarly when we deny the sentence. If we think of words and sentences as classes of noises and marks, then we may say that words and sentences are 'physical' ('nonpsychological') phenomena. But we must not suppose the meaning of words and sentences to be a property which they have apart from their relations to the psychological attitudes of the people who *use* them . . . . A word or sentence designates so-and-so only if people *use* it to designate so-and-so.[2]

Here Chisholm justifies his theory of "semantic" reference — the theory that a linguistic expression can refer without implication of

[1] Chisholm (1957), Ch. 11.
[2] *Ibid.*, p. 174—5.

existence – by appeal to a theory of "personal" reference, *viz.*, that it is we, the language-users, who *do* the referring. We might remark here that Chisholm's notion of reference is compatible with Frege's notion of (semantic) reference which admits names that do not refer to anything. We will see, moreover, in Chapter VI, how Chisholm's account echoes that of Husserl's theory of linguistic reference which tells us that it is an intentional act which "animates" the mere physical signs or sounds making them vehicles of reference.

Chisholm goes on to argue that we cannot replace talk about a word's "designating" or "referring" by talk about some object's satisfying the intension of a certain word or predicate. For the adequacy of this kind of account is tested by the willingness or preparedness of some language-user, A, to utter a word or assent to it under certain conditions. Now, either we describe this situation of A's readiness to ascribe the word or predicate to some object on a particular occasion in terms of A's *beliefs* – in which case we re-introduce intentionality – or we describe the situation in purely physicalistic terms as a situation of response to a stimulus. The latter involves talking about purely physical events and states of affairs. Chisholm argues that attempts to do this inevitably fail. A's readiness to ascribe some word 'P' to some object, O, can never be reduced to a case of response to a stimulus. For ascribing a word to an object involves A's "taking something to be" a ϕ. Consistency of A's responses to certain stimuli can tell us, of certain things, *that* A takes them to be ϕ. But, of any of these things, it cannot tell us when A does *not* take it to be ϕ.

For Chisholm, then, talk about the psychological cannot be replaced by talk about the non-psychological, such as talk about linguistic behaviour, physical states, responses to stimuli: This implies and is implied by the fact that intentional constructions cannot be translated into non-intentional constructions.

The problem for the irreducibility theorist is to provide an analysis of those psychological acts which are directed to an existing object without thereby losing sight of the intentionality of the sentences we use to talk about them: Is it possible to assert that the objects of such acts are real, existing objects, while at the same time preserving the intentionality of sentences about those acts?

The irreducibility theorists insist that "A's thinking of Y is the same sort of thing whether Y exists or not" – Prior's third clause. Existence or non-existence of the object is irrelevant to the truth of a sentence about A's thinking of some object, Y. A's thinking of an existing Y submits to the same kind of analysis as A's thinking of a non-existing Y. Sentences about either of these activities have the form of A thinks $(\exists x) \ldots x \ldots$. Thus for a sentence of the form, A thinks that $(\exists x) \ldots x \ldots$, on the irreducibility view, there may be a true substitution-instance of the quantified formula which occurs *within* the scope of the psychological verb. Existence of the object thought about cannot mean that "A thinks of some object, Y" is to be analysed as $(\exists x) \ x$ is thought of by A, as the relational theorists insist.

What this means is that for the irreducibility theorists, the expression "what can be thought about" is interpreted in such a way that anything whatsoever can be thought about. When Anscombe[3] says that she uses the expression "object of thought" in the "old" sense, she means precisely this. The "old" sense of "object of thought" is the sense in which we say of all psychological acts that they are directed to some *object*. The sense of "object of thought" here is therefore Brentano's sense. By contrast, Russell's sense of "object of thought" is the sense in which only existing things – or things known infallibly to exist – could be called an "object of thought" or what's thought "about". So, on Anscombe's view, sentences about existing objects of thought are to be analysed in the same way as sentences about non-existing objects of thought, *viz.*, in the form of $A \ \phi$'s that $(\exists x) \ldots x \ldots$.

§2. *Anscombe's theory of intentional objects*

Anscombe conflates intentionality with a "t" with intensionality with an "s" saying that the differences in spelling are the result of Sir William Hamilton's idea of transforming the old logical word "intention" into one that "looked more like 'extension'."[4] Anscombe is in fact mistaken in thinking this. As William Kneale points out: "In Hamilton's usage 'intension' had nothing at all to

[3] Anscombe (1965).
[4] *Ibid.*, p. 159.

do with 'intention', being merely a rather unfortunate substitute for the word 'comprehension', which the Port Royal logicians used for the range of attributes signified by a general term in distinction from the extension or range of examples to which it might be applied truly".[5] Anscombe's choice of the "older spelling" of intension with a "t" is significant, however.

Anscombe regards "intention" and its cognates as a *logical* notion, but prefers this "older" spelling because "the word is the same as the one in common use in connexion with action".[6] It is because the same concept occurs in relation to saying, i.e., to language, that we can "make the bridge to the logician's use".[7]

Thus for Anscombe, the *logical* features which constitute the intentionality of sentences derive from her philosophical psychology. Specifically, these features derive from what Anscombe sees as the distinctive features of intentionalness in action. These are as follows:

(i) Descriptions under which you intend to do what you do may not come true. Anscombe's example is that of a slip of the tongue or pen.

(ii) The description under which you intend what you do may be vague or indeterminate. For example, you mean to put the book on the table, but not to put it anywhere in particular on the table. However, in putting the book on the table, you do put it in a particular spot.

(iii) Not any description of what you do describes it as the action you intended: only under certain of its descriptions will it be intentional.

Analogous features are to be found in the case of sentences which are intentional. Anscombe is talking here about sentences whose

[5] Kneale (1968), p. 84. Kneale goes on to say: "Hamilton's new word and his associated doctrine of the inverse variation of intension and extension were both suggested to him by a passing remark of Cajetan that there is an extensive sense in which a genus may be said to have a greater collective |power than a species, because it contains more members, and an intensive sense in which a species may be said to have a greater collective power than a genus, because it unites its members more closely" (Hamilton's *Lectures on Logic*, vol. I, p. 141). These remarks serve to distance Hamilton's original notion of "intension" from that of the post-Russellian philosophers like Quine and Putnam for whom "intensions" are said to be "mental entities". *Infra,* Chapter V.

[6] Anscombe (1965), p. 159.

[7] *Ibid.*

verb takes an object or object-phrase. Features analogous to those above are to be found in relation to the descriptions occurring as object-words or phrases of intentional sentences of this kind. These features are:

(i′) The possible non-existence of the object: Because sentences like "X thought of ____" and "X worships ____" do not require completion with the name of something real in order to be true, they are not to be assimilated to sentences like "X bit ____" which must, if true, be completed by adding the name of something real.

(ii′) The possible indeterminacy of the object: "I can think of a man without thinking of a man of any particular height; I cannot hit a man without hitting a man of some particular height".[8]

(iii′) Non-substitutability of different descriptions of the object, where it does exist.

These are, for Anscombe, the criteria for the intentionality of sentences.

Before considering Anscombe's criteria for intentionality, it is important to examine the origins of these criteria in those features of intentionalness of action which have been stated above. The characteristics (i)–(iii) have been selected on the basis of a certain way of analysing descriptions of intentional actions. Each of them implies a constrast between

(a) a description under which I intend to do x; and
(b) a description which is true of x,

where "x" is something that I do. This mode of analysis is motivated by considerations of a straightforwardly Cartesian kind: Knowledge of my intentions – expressed by (a) – is not based on observation, and is something to which I have "privileged access"; knowledge of what is getting done – expressed by (b) – is based on observation, and is something that is publicly accessible. In short, intentional action – "what I am doing" – is analysable in terms of a "private" and a "public" component. This Cartesian-inspired analysis gives us what is peculiar to intentional action. At the same time however this kind of analysis imposes serious constraints of an epistemological kind on our understanding of

[8] *Ibid.*, p. 161.

"intentional action". Dónnellan,[9] for example, shows that reports of one's own intentional actions (of the kind expressed in (a) above) cannot be assimilated to the standard models of Cartesian "knowledge without observation". For the standard models, which are first-person reports of psychological states or of kinaesthetic sensations, display not only non-observational knowledge but immunity to error as well. But reports of one's own intentional actions display the seemingly incompatible features of being known non-observationally, and, at the same time, being open to the possibility of error. However these features are incompatible only from the standpoint of Descartes' dualistic epistemological framework. The intentionality of action cannot be accommodated within such a framework.

One way of releasing intentionality from the constraints of such a framework, it would seem, is to characterise intentionality as a logical feature of language rather than as a psychological feature of action. This means that considerations of an epistemological kind are replaced by considerations concerning the logical features of language. Moreover, it looks as though the *dualism* of the Cartesian epistemological framework can be undercut, for it is precisely the intentionality of e.g., "perceives", which allows us to say that the object of perception is some real, existing thing, and not some purely mental item to which we have privileged access. However − to anticipate a fundamental difficulty in Anscombe's account − the characteristics of the intentionality of language derive from those features of intentionalness in action which are themselves a product of a dualistic analysis of intentionalness in action. This dualism persists in Anscombe's account of the intentionality of language but not at any overt level. The distinction exploited by Anscombe between "intentional objects" and "material objects" bears no resemblance to a dualism of the incorrigibly and the corrigibly known, the privately and the publicly accessible, or of inner and outer realms. It is, rather, a distinction designed to cut across any of these dualisms. However, it is in the very setting up of the problems of intentionality that certain dichotomies are imported. The puzzles surrounding intentionality arise because intentionality cannot be accommodated into any of these imported dichotomies.

[9] Donnellan (1963).

Our general problem concerns objective reference in the case of those intentional activities which are directed to an existing object. In Anscombe's case, this is the problem of ensuring that the *objects* of such acts are not appearances or some kind of counterpart to the real thing, without thereby losing sight of the intentionality of the *act*. The problem of objective reference is most acute in the case of those "sensation-verbs" exemplified by the verb "perceives" in that sense which necessitates that there be some real, existing object. For sentences containing "perceives" must, on Anscombe's account, still be intentional.

As Anscombe sees it, a satisfactory account of the intentionality of perception must incorporate the insights of both realist and sense-impression theories, but must exclude what she takes to be incorrect in each of these doctrines. Anscombe introduces her notions of "intentional objects" and "material objects" to help provide such an account. The puzzles that arise from her account of intentionality are, however, traceable to the kinds of distinctions operative in the doctrines of both realism and sense-impression theories — these distinctions are imported into Anscombe's setting up of the problem.

I shall conclude the present discussion by considering the way in which Anscombe states the problem of objective reference and by outlining her grammatical criteria for intentionality. We can then turn to an analysis of Anscombe's thesis concerning the intentionality of "perceives" and an examination of the puzzles that surround her thesis. In the course of this, I shall make explicit some of the fundamental distinctions which are responsible for these puzzles.

The problem of objective reference first emerges in Anscombe's discussion of the criterion of possible non-existence of the object. Sentences about psychological acts, like sentences about physical acts, have the form of a predicate expression and two referring expressions: $X \phi$'s Y. The problem about "objects of thought" is the problem about what kinds of thing can be picked out by "Y" in this formula if the predicate "ϕ" designates some psychological act. The truth of a sentence about a physical act, "X bit _____", demands that the name of something real be inserted in the blank. This is not the case with sentences like "X thinks of _____" or "X worships _____". Vacuous names may fill the blank in these last two sentences. But when the name of something real does fill the blank in a true sentence like "X thinks of ___" then "it is the real thing itself, not some intermediary, that X thought of".[10] When thinking, worshipping, etc., are directed to an existing object, then the object of thought, worship, etc., is precisely that real, existing thing that one might also kick, bite, hit, etc.

What Anscombe wants to resist, here, is the suggestion that an object of thought is some mere idea, mental image or ghostly counterpart of the real thing. If it is an idea or mental image which constitutes the object of thought in X's thinking about some non-existing Y, then we must, to be consistent, say that it is an idea or image which constitutes the object of X's thought when he is thinking about some *existing* Y. But this is clearly false in that, if I am thinking of Winston Churchill, then it is the real existing individual which I am thinking of, and not some idea of him. The same point can be made in a different way. As Prior, quoting Reid, says: ". . . it is surely obvious . . . that to think of X is one thing and to think of an idea or image of X is another thing, and the difference is especially obvious when X itself doesn't exist but the idea or image does".[11]

For Anscombe, "intentional object" is a grammatical notion: Intentional objects are a sub-class of grammatical direct objects. The notion of "(grammatical) direct object" is explicated in terms of the grammatical understanding displayed in giving the direct object of a sentence such as "John gave Mary a book". Here, the question, "What is the direct object of the verb of this sentence?" is equivalent to the question, "What does the sentence say John gave Mary?" Grammatical understanding of "direct object" is displayed by the "special use" of the phrase, "a book", when it is used in response to this question. By "special use" here Anscombe means that the phrase "a book", as answer to the question, does not name a bit of language, nor something that language stands for. Intentional objects are a sub-class of such objects.

Intentional objects are contrasted with material objects. The contrast is made in the following way: X aims at something which he takes to be a stag, but which is, in fact, his father. We can describe this act by a sentence of the form, "X aimed at ___".

[10] Anscombe (1965), p. 161.
[11] Prior (1971), p. 129.

If the blank is filled in by a description under which X aimed at something – *viz*., the phrase, "a stag", – then this phrase gives us the intentional object of X's aiming. But there is a sense in which the sentence "X aimed at his father" is true. Here the blank is filled in by a description which is true of the object aimed at. Phrases giving a description true of the object ϕ'd, where "ϕ's" is an intentional verb, are said to give the material object of ϕ-ing. When X aims at something which does not in fact exist – e.g., an hallucinatory stag – then there is an intentional object of his aiming, but no material object. If, still in this totally hallucinatory scene, X, in fact shoots his father, this would not make his father the material object of his aiming. For a material object is given by a description which is true of *what is ϕ'd* – that is to say, true of the intentional object. Finally, where X aims at something which he takes to be his father and which is in fact his father, then, in the sentence, "X aimed at his father", the phrase "his father" gives us both the intentional object and the material object of his aiming. But this cannot mean that intentional object and material object are one and the same thing. For the sentence necessarily has an intentional object, but only contingently a material object. Thus, the more appropriate way of stating this is to say that the intentional object "aligns with"[12] the material object.

We are now in a position to see how Anscombe proposes to deal with the problem of objective reference in the case of those intentional acts which are directed to an existing object. The problem is one concerning the relation between intentional and material objects. In particular, it is the puzzles surrounding the intentionality of sensation-verbs like "perceives" which create the *problem*. As mentional earlier, Anscombe does not provide a solution to the problem. She only succeeds in setting the problem up. In the course of discussing the way in which Anscombe sets up the problem of the intentionality of sensation, I propose to make explicit some of the presupposition involved.

---

[12] This is not Anscombe's way of characterising the relation between intentional and material object – the problem is that Anscombe does not (and, as we will see, cannot) offer us a satisfactory account of how the two are related. This characterisation does, however, serve a useful intuitive purpose of preserving the relevant differences and similarities between the intentional and material object in the case of this particular example.

§3. *The intentionality of perception*

In the case of "perceives", Anscombe's notions of intentional and material objects are introduced to perform a variety of tasks.

First, they are designed to capture the "transparency" of perception and, thereby to preserve the distinction between veridical and non-veridical perceptual experiences. "Transparency" of perception here means "perceives" in the sense which necessitates the existence of some object. If the transparency of perception is not insisted upon, then there can be no distinction between veridical and mistaken perceptual experiences — a distinction we *must* preserve if we are to claim that perception, a psychological act, is capable of objective reference.

Second, the distinction between intentional and material objects is introduced to capture what is correct in the doctrines of sense-impression theories and realism: Sense-impression theorists are correct in insisting that, in the case of any sensation (i.e., perception), there is always a describable sense-impression. This view acknowledges the "sensation-aspect" of "perceives". Realists are correct in insisting that there is a sense in which the truth of a perceptual claim depends upon contextual features — i.e., that there exist the object claimed to be perceived. This view acknowledges the "epistemic" aspect of "perceives". Anscombe's account of intentionality in terms of intentional and material objects is designed to capture both of these aspects of "perceives", and hence to legitimise the two uses of perceives — its use in describing mere sense-impressions, and its use in describing what is claimed to really exist.

I turn now to an analysis of Anscombe's arguments concerning the intentionality of "perceives".

(1) There is always an intentional object of perceiving. Sense-impression theorists such as Berkeley,[13] and realists (amongst whom Anscombe seems to include ordinary-language philosophers like G. E. Moore and Rylean behaviourists) fail, in their different ways, to acknowledge the intentionality of perception: Sense-impression theorists "misconstrue intentional objects as

---

[13] Russell's "sense-data" theory of perceiving is, for Anscombe, included amongst the sense-impression theories. Anscombe (1965), p. 169.

material objects of sensation";[14] realist philosophers "allow only material objects of sensation". Anscombe, however, wants to retain what she sees as being correct in each of these views. Sense-impression theorists are correct in claiming that there is always some content of a person's visual experience: The dictum, "He who sees must see something",[15] is true if it is taken to mean just this. Anscombe re-expresses this as the thesis that there is always an intentional object of perceiving.

(2) There *is* such a thing as the material use of "perceives".[16] In this the realists are correct: There is a sense of "perceives" according to which it is appropriate to say, "You couldn't have *seen* a unicorn; unicorns don't exist". Taken this way, perception is held to be "transparent" (in a sense to be explained, below). Non-existence of the object is an objection to the truth of a claim to have perceived that object. The material use of "perceives" is the use which demands a material object. If I use "perceives" materially in "I perceive a tree", then I intend the words "a tree" as giving the *material object* of my perceiving.

(3) "Perceives" may have a merely intentional use.[17] In the sentence, "I perceive a tree", I *may* be using "perceives" in its merely intentional sense. In this case, I intend the words "a tree" as a description of "what-appears-to-me" — that is, a description of my sense-impression. The idealists are correct, insofar as there is such a thing as describing sense-impressions, and moreover these descriptions may be quite varied and diverse. There may be a number of different descriptions that I can give of any one sense-impression.

(4) The material use of "perceives" is its primary use.[18] The material use of "perceives" is the use most often intended. But, more importantly, the material use is *epistemologically prior* to its merely intentional use. Ordinary-language philosophers are correct in claiming that descriptions of appearances-to-me are derivative from descriptions of things as they really are: Our understanding of a description-of-an-appearance presupposes our understanding of a description of *what* an appearance is *of.*

[14] *Ibid.*
[15] *Ibid.*, pp. 173–4.
[16] *Ibid.*, p. 171.
[17] *Ibid.*, p. 174.
[18] *Ibid.*, p. 172.

(5) The test of whether "perceives" is being used materially or in its merely intentional sense is the preparedness of the user to withdraw his claim to have "perceived *o*" when confronted with evidence of the non-existence of "*o*".[19]

I have introduced into this analysis two notions which require further elaboration: The "transparency" of perception and the "epistemological priority" of the material use of "perceives".

The problem of the intentionality of perception is the problem of preserving both (a) the transparency of perception, and (b) the intentionality of perception. The "transparency" of perception, here, cannot mean Quine's "logical transparency" for this characterisation excludes the possibility of ascribing intentionality to "perceives". If a context is *logically* transparent, then none of Chisholm's criteria for intentionality is satisfied. To distinguish the transparency of perception in Anscombe's characterisation, I shall introduce the term, "psychologically transparent". To say that perception is *psychologically* transparent is to affirm that there must exist some object but to deny that different descriptions of the object can be substituted for one another, *salva veritate.* It follows from this that perception is intentional by virtue of Chisholm's (and Anscombe's) third criterion of non-subsitutivity.[20]

We have already seen how the thesis of the *logical transparency* of perception endorsed by extensionalist theories, such as those of Russell and Quine, means that sentences about perceiving carry existential implication *and* admit substitutivity. The thesis of the *psychological transparency* of perception, on the other hand, tells us that sentences about "perceives" which imply existence need not be extensional, that is, admit substitutivity. The difference between these two ways of characterising the "transparency" of perception results from the different kinds of analyses which

[19] *Ibid.*, pp. 171–2.
[20] We can disregard here (a) Chisholm's second criteria of lack of implication of truth or falsity, for it is inapplicable to the kinds of sentences we are talking about, i.e., sentences which take a direct object. Moreover we can, for the moment, disregard (b) Anscombe's second criterion of possible indeterminacy. For if a sentence satisfies *this* criterion, it is *ipso facto* intentional by her third criterion of non-substitutivity: From the truth of "I perceive a leafy tree" we cannot infer "I perceive a tree with 5,839 leaves even though the latter, simply by describing further determinations of the object perceived, is true of that object.

are seen to be appropriate for sentences about perceiving. If "*A* perceives *o*" is taken to imply something of the form:

$(\exists x)\, x$ is perceived by A,

then it follows that perceiving is logically transparent. (The sentence admits substitutivity). If the same sentence, "*A* perceives *o*", is taken to imply something of the form:

A perceives that $(\exists x)\, x \ldots$,

then it follows that perceiving is psychologically transparent: There may be a true substitution-instance of the formula (i.e., the object perceived may exist), but the sentence does not admit substitutivity.

We must now look to the motivation for treating perception as psychologically transparent.

If we take perception to be psychologically transparent, then we use the verb "perceives" in the sense which necessitates that there exist some real object. Non-existence of the object will be an objection to the truth of any sentence containing "perceives". Any true sentence containing "perceives" will therefore be a sentence about a veridical perceptual experience. If my "perceptual" experience is non-veridical — if I claim to perceive an X when, in fact, there exists no X — then the sentence I use to report this claim will be false. What this means is that my claim to perceive X (when the experience is non-veridical) is a *mistaken* claim. Only veridical experiences constitute a genuine claim of "perceiving X"; non-veridical experiences constitute a mistaken claim of "perceiving X".

This means that, if we subscribe to the view that perception is "transparent", we thereby assert (a) the primacy of veridical perceptual experiences: Only veridical perceptions are genuine cases of "perceiving X"; and, (b) this is an *epistemological* priority. To explain this more fully, we must recall our earlier discussion concerning the difference between real and imagined objects of intentional acts.

I can distinguish between an idea (or image) of x and a real x. At this phenomenological level, the distinction between the real x and an idea of x is epistemologically neutral. The questions,

How do I know that this is the real x? or How do I know that this is an idea (or image) of x? have not been introduced.

But given a particular experience, e.g., of perceiving x, we can raise the question, How do I know that it's the *real x*? This question is motivated by straightforwardly Cartesian considerations: Given that there are real things *and* ideas or images of those things, and given that there can be ideas and images *without* there being any real thing, the idea or the image can be a source of error. Therefore, how can I be sure that my experience is in fact an experience of a real – i.e. existing – object? Here, "attaining" *only* the image or the idea constitutes error; "attaining" the real constitutes knowledge. Therefore, epistemological priority is conferred upon attainment of the real. Anscombe's way of distinguishing between the idea and the real involves this assumption which, it would seem, is unneccesary, as the distinction can be drawn phenomenologically, on the basis of a more neutral set of assumptions.

It would be misleading to say that Anscombe and others are importing Descartes' epistemological dualism into accounts of the intentionality of perception by subscribing to the view that perception is psychologically transparent. (In fact, as mentioned earlier, by a commitment to just this account of perception, Cartesian dualism seems to be undermined). However in accepting the epistemological priority of veridical perception, Anscombe is in fact importing (i) that Cartesian-derived contrast of the image or idea *as opposed to* the real, and (ii) the association of the idea/image with the *possibility of error*. To demonstrate this: hallucinatory experiences are not just intentional acts in their own right — they are also cases of *mistaken* perceptual claims. This is what the distinction between veridical and non-veridical "perceptual" experiences consists in.

But we must ask: How is it that Anscombe's account comes to import (i) a contrast of image/idea as opposed to the real, and (ii) an association of image/idea with error? There are two ways in which these implications enter: First, Anscombe's identification of "merely intentional" object with that which sense-impression theorists take to be the object of sensation, (*viz.*, sense-impressions: The sense-impression theorist "misconstrues *intentional objects* (given by descriptions of *sense-impressions*) as material objects of sensation").[21] Second, Anscombe's insistence on the primacy of the material use of "perceives" where this "primacy" turns out to be *epistemological priority*. I shall deal with each of these below.

When I use "perceives" in its merely intentional sense, I do not intend the sentence containing this verb as giving the material object of my perceiving. I intend the sentence as giving only a description of my sense-impression. If however I use the word materially, then I intend the sentence as giving the material object of my perceiving. The test of whether or not I am using "perceives" one way or the other is my preparedness to withdraw my claim to have perceived x when I learn of the non-existence of x. The merely intentional use of "perceives", then, is clearly different from the material use of "perceives". Moreover the truth-conditions for the sentence "I perceive o" or "A perceives o" will vary according to whether the verb is intended materially or not. But the notions of "merely intentional use" and "material use" of "perceives" cannot be understood independently of one another. When "perceives" is used materially, there *is* an intentional object of perception – this is demanded by (1) above, and we will be discussing this later. When "perceives" is used in its "merely" intentional sense, then it is used in a sense which can constitute a case of mistaken perception by the standards of the material use of the verb. Now, the "merely intentional" use of "perceives" must *necessarily* be characterised as a use which carries the possibility of error, because the material use of "perceives" is the *primary* use: that is to say, it is in relation to the material use of "perceives" that the "merely intentional" use is defined. The material use of "perceives" is the use which corresponds to the doctrine of the transparency of perception. It is the sense in which non-existence of the object constitutes an objection to the truth of the sentence containing that verb. In asserting the primacy of this use of "perceives", one thereby asserts the epistemological priority of veridical perception. In relation to this use of "perceives", any claim to perceive some object, x, where x does not exist is a mistaken claim. "Merely intentional" uses of "perceives" are those uses which do not require the existence of the object, in which case, by the standards of the material use of that same word, they involve mistaken claims to "perceive" (taken materially).

[21] *Ibid.*, p. 169.

So, by asserting the primacy of the material use of "perceives" in a way which implies the epistemological priority of veridical perception, one thereby admits (i) a Cartesian-derived kind of contrast between the object of the merely intentional use of "perceives" on the one hand, and the object of "perceives" used materially, on the other. The former stands opposed to the latter as mere sense-impression to really existing thing (in just the same way as we saw in the opposition of image/idea to the real), precisely because of (ii) the Cartesian-derived association of sense-impressions with the possibility of error: We can't *just* admit sense-impressions as the only legitimate objects of all perceivings (the merely intentional use is not the only use). But, if we admit really existing objects as the legitimate objects of some perceptual claims, *and* in addition give priority to such claims (assert the primacy of the material use), then sense-impressions must be regarded as sources of possible error where these latter, superior claims are concerned.

I have deliberately refrained here from equating Anscombe's "intentional objects" with sense-impressions, and her "material objects" with real, existing things: if this were so then there would be no need to introduce a "grammatical" notion of "intentional object". There is however some equivocation in Anscombe's use of these terms. This is because, when "perceives" is used in its *"merely* intentional sense", the words giving the object of this verb give what the sense-impression theorists take to be the object of "perceives", *tout court, viz.,* they describe an impression. But, if we are to shed what is said to be incorrect about sense-impression theories of perceptual objects, impressions must be understood as "mere" impressions — that which is contrastable with the real. It seems legitimate to infer from this (a) that the *intentional object* of "perceives", when it is used *merely* intentionally is given by a description of an impression; and (b) that intentional objects are contrastable with — i.e., opposed to — the object of "perceives" when the verb is used materially.

This move *looks* to be legitimate because, in introducing the sense-impression theorists' notion of "impression" and the realist-inspired qualification of this as *"mere* impression", we are thereby importing the dualistic framework of appearance vs reality against which the notion of "impression" or "mere impression" is set. But the move *cannot* be a legitimate one, for when "perceives" is used materially, there *is* still an intentional object, and *this* cannot be a sense-impression in addition to the real thing. It is here that some of the puzzles concerning intentionality have their origin: "Intentionality" which is at once equated with a dualistically-based notion of "impression" or "appearance-to-me", is at the same time, given the responsibility for cutting through this very dualism – for in cases of veridical perception, when "perceives" is used materially in a sentence that is true, there must still be an intentional object.

§4. *Perception and its puzzles*

There is another reason why "intentionality", characterised as a grammatical notion contrastable with material objects, cannot be made to fit the framework shared by sense-impression theorists and realists. A material object is not some really, existing thing nor, as we shall see later, is it that which is given by a description of what really exists. If the sentence "I perceive X" reports a veridical perception, we don't say that the words giving the object of my perceiving give only a material object. Rather, for Anscombe, intentional and material object somehow "align with" one another in this case. This means that the question of "objective reference" in the case of veridical perceivings are really questions about the relation between the intentional and the material object of "perceives".

In considering this question, we are considering cases of perception which are psychologically transparent: that is, cases where there is necessarily some existing object. Let us take, as an example, a situation where some person, A, sees cattle in a paddock and takes them to be sheep. A reports his experience as follows: "I perceive sheep". If "perceives" is intended in its material use by A, then that sentence is false. Correspondingly, the sentence "A perceives cattle" is true. In this case, A's claim is mistaken; the mistake consists in his giving a description which is false of what is perceived. But if, in uttering the original sentence, A intends "perceives" in its merely intentional sense, then "A perceives sheep" is true; the sentence "A perceives cattle" if false.

This makes it look as though there is an epistemological gap between intentional and material objects. Moreover, this gap seems to consist in precisely that kind of epistemological distinction that led to Donnellan's puzzles about intention and action: If "perceives" is used materially, then first-person authority is absent; if "perceives" is used intentionally, then third-person authority is absent. The difference in truth-conditions for material uses of "perceives" as opposed to merely intentional uses of "perceives" *seems* to amount to a difference in the epistemological principles that are appealed to in each of these cases. What prevents us from levelling this sort of objection to Anscombe's account of the distinction between intentional and material objects is, however, something which is a source of some of the more intractable puzzles about the intentionality of "perceives": This is her statement that a material object is given by *a description which is true of what is perceived.* The fundamental difficulty here is in giving content to the notion of "what is perceived".

Anscombe attempts to deal with this difficulty by asking, When does a description give a material object of seeing?

First, a material object of seeing can't be given by a description of what is before my eyes when they are open and I am seeing. For, if I am hallucinating, then in no sense do I *see* what is before my eyes. We can recall here her earlier example of the hallucinating aimer who shoots his father; here, the father is not the material object of aiming.

Second, a description which is true of what is seen but which doesn't give what is seen, gives *only* a material object of seeing: For example, "I saw a man born in Jerusalem" said of someone seen in Oxford whose birth I had not witnessed, may give a description true of what is seen but in no sense gives what is seen.[22] The description is non-intentional. This is different from the case of seeing a tomato, where it might be argued that the words "a tomato" describe something I couldn't have *seen*, for a tomato has a back side which no single view of the object can give. Anscombe argues that seeing a man who was born in Jerusalem is different from the case of seeing a tomato, for "if you look at a tomato and take only a single view you *must* see what *might*

[22] *Ibid.*, pp. 176–7.

be only half a tomato: that is what seeing a tomato is".[23] So, whereas the words "a man born in Jerusalem" give only a material object of seeing, the words "a tomato" (in "I see a tomato") give an *intentional* as well as a material object of seeing.

But none of these examples tells us what a description which gives a material object is a description *of*.

Third, a material object of seeing can't be given by a description which gives the intentional object of some *other* act. For example, a material object of aiming can't be given by a description which gives *only* the intentional object of some other act, i.e., seeing. For if something is *only* an intentional object of seeing, how can it possibly be a material object of some other act — aiming? This particular puzzle arises from Anscombe's insistence that the material use of "perceives" is the primary use. Thus "what is *only* an intentional object" is equated with "mere impression". And the opposition between "mere impressions" and what is given by a description of the object of "perceives" in its material sense, is, as we have seen, an epistemologically based one.

Finally, we cannot say that we have a material object of seeing only if some intentional description is also true of what really, physically exists. For I may see my watch, but see it only as a shiny blur. In this case, the words "a shiny blur" are not true of anything that physically exists in the context, but they may be the only description I have of what I see.

We can summarise these puzzles in the following way: A material object of seeing is given by a description which is true of *what is seen*. Here the words, "what is seen" cannot mean (i) something which physically exists and is before my eyes when they are open; (ii) something, like a man's being born in Jerusalem which, in the circumstances, I couldn't have *seen*; (iii) something which is given by a merely intentional description of the object of this or any other act; (iv) some physically existing thing of which some intentional description is true.

These puzzles are generated because in the examples discussed there is a demand that the material object of seeing be something that is non-intentionally characterisable, and it is impossible for Anscombe's notion of "material object" as

---

[23] *Ibid.*, p. 177.

"that-which-is-given-by-a-description-which-is-true-of-*what-is-seen*"
to satisfy this demand. The *demand* arises from the assumption
that in merely intentional uses of "perceives" the words which
describe the object describe merely what-appear-to-me. The things
that are characterised intentionally are *mere* appearances. Mere
appearances which are the objects of purely intentional uses of
"perceives" must be contrastable with the objects of the material
use of "perceives". The material use of "perceives" is epistemologically prior to the merely intentional use. Therefore the contrast between the objects of perception in each case must be a
contrast between "what is a mere impression and carries the
possibility of error" as opposed to "what is *not* a mere impression
and carries veridicalness". Only the latter can be that which
constitutes the material object of "perceives". But, by the same
token, the latter can only be given by a description that is non-
intentional. The demand is, therefore, that the material object be
something which is non-intentionally characterisable. For what
is characterised purely intentionally is the mere appearance.
Anscombe's notion of "material object" cannot satisfy this
demand, for although "perceives" has a material object, perception
is nonetheless intentional.

We can see this demand in the way that the preceding problems
have been set up: a material object of seeing can't be dissociated
from the intentional object of seeing, for it is not *just* a real
physical, existing thing. If we don't accept this then we dispense
with the intentionality of perception. On the other hand, a
material object can't be parasitic on the intentional object. Material
objects must be contrasted with mere impressions, but must not
be assimilated to the category of real, independently existing,
physical things. But the dualistic constraints of opposing the
"mere impression" to "the real" don't allow for any other alternative.

It seems to me that Anscombe's insight that the intentionality
of perception must be retained is correct. However, she is mistaken
in seeing the alternative – that the material object must be parasitic
on the intentional object – as the *only* other alternative. The
implication of insisting that this *is* the only other alternative is
that the intentional cannot be *a means to* the material object. We
can demonstrate this by recalling Anscombe's remarks concerning

an act of perceiving a tomato. What's given to me in a single perceiving of a tomato (i.e., the *intentional* object of my perceiving) *must* be something which *might* be only half a tomato. The intentional object of my perceiving here is, in other words, something which admits the possibility of error in my claim to perceive "a tomato". And this possibility cannot be avoided. For *seeing* a tomato consists just *in* seeing what might be half a tomato.

When we turn to the phenomenological approach to intentionality in Chapter VI, we will see that a quite different account can be given of the relation between intentional objects and what Anscombe calls material objects in the kind of example discussed above. To anticipate: The single perception of the tomato is but one of a whole network of acts which, taken together, "intend" the "real" object. The details of such an account must be postponed until later, but the immediate point I wish to make is this: The single perception of a tomato *does* give only a "half-tomato view". But this need not be regarded solely as a "possibly-mistaken" perception. It can instead be regarded as just one of many perceptions which constitute the *means to* understanding what "perceiving a tomato" in its material sense consists in. But, as we will see later, *this* way of understanding the relation between what Anscombe calls "intentional" and "material" objects requires an appeal to a three-levelled semantical framework.

The constraints of the dualistic framework which is implicit in Anscombe's discussion of intentionality become clear, when we see that the possibility of treating intentionality as *a means to* objective reference (whether we construe this as "the real" or as "that which is given by a material object") is ruled out. The intentional is, as it were, a possible barrier to achieving objective reference. This is so because the "merely intentional" is associated with possibility of error — an association which is demanded if we are to preserve the distinction between veridical and non-veridical "perceivings", by insisting on the epistemological priority of the material use of "perceives". Accordingly, cases of hallucinating, imagining, experiencing illusions, become cases of *failed* or *mistaken* "perception". So on Anscombe's account, what we have been describing in metaphysically-neutral terms as "objective reference" in the case of intentional verbs like "perceives", comes to be associated with the epistemological priority of veridical perception.

§5. *Concluding remarks*

The problem with which we began in Chapter III is that of characterising "objective reference" in the case of those psychological acts exemplified by X's thinking of an existing Y. For the relational theorists, to say of such an act that it succeeds in achieving objective reference is to say that the sentence "X thinks of Y" which describes that act is an extensional sentence. This means a denial of the intentionality of those acts or, on the more extreme consequence of this theory, a denial of the intentionality of any "psychological" acts.

On the irreducibility theory discussed in this chapter, the sentence, "X thinks of Y" is always intentional whether or not Y exists: "The mere fact of real existence ... can't make so very much difference to the analysis of a sentence like 'X thought of ____'".[24] But clearly, for Anscombe, the "mere fact of real existence" of the object of thought is of *some* significance, for it is the source of her problems in providing such an analysis. When Y *does* exist (in X's thinking of Y), the object of thought is nothing other than, or in addition to, the real existing thing which might also be the object of a physical act. An existing object of thought is a material object, where the latter is defined as that which is given by a description which is true of what is thought. However, there seems to be no coherent account that we can give of what such a description is a description *of*. For, if thinking, aiming, perceiving, etc., (when directed to some real object) always have an *intentional* object, there seems to be no satisfactory way of characterising the independent *reality* of the objects of these acts.

The crucial advantage of the linguistic version of the intentionality thesis seemed to consist in the fact that psychological activities, because they are intentional, could be seen as capable of objective reference.[25] Intentional acts and their objects are not,

[24] *Ibid.*, p. 161.
[25] *Supra*, Ch. I, §1.

as Brentano believed, "intra-mental" relations and objects, sealed off against the real or external world. At the same time, however, this thesis means that the very concept of "the mental" as that which is characterised by intentionality is threatened. For when we explicate what the "capacity for objective reference" consists in, then either (i) we are compelled to dismiss "the psychological" altogether, in the manner of Russell and Quine, or (ii) if we wish to retain the autonomy of the psychological, like Chisholm and Anscombe, then we face the seemingly intractable problem of preserving both the "reality" of the object and the intentionality of the act.

It is ironic that, in stating the problem of intentionality in this way, the difficulties that beset Brentano's original version of the intentionality thesis seem to re-emerge. Brentano, like Anscombe, was unable to combine an account of the object-directedness of mental acts with a satisfactory account of the status of those objects. And finally, as in the case of Russell, Quine, etc., he was forced to abandon the doctrine of intentionality altogether. The similarities between Brentano's problem of intentionality and problems surrounding its linguistic re-formulation can only be drawn at a superficial level. The reasons for Brentano's difficulties, and the problematic within which he attempted to remove these difficulties are significantly distanced from the factors which lead to the puzzles concerning the linguistic version of the intentionality thesis. Most importantly, it is no longer Brentano's notion of "the mental" (i.e., mental phenomena) to which intentionality is ascribed. The contrast of sentences about psychological phenomena and sentences about non-psychological phenomena is not just an analogue of Brentano's dualistic contrast of mental as opposed to physical phenomena. In fact it constitutes a denial of that kind of dualism espoused by Brentano, which sustains a notion of "the mental" as that which is hermetically sealed off against "the real". In ascribing intentionality to *sentences* about the psychological we break through this dualism, for the language that we use to talk about the mental — i.e., psychological — can succeed in achieving reference to objects which are not "mental entities".

The theories that we have been discussing in Chapters III and IV are motivated by a shared concern to undercut a dualism of mental and physical phenomena: That is, the postulation of two mutually exclusive classes of phenomena — the mental and the physical — conceived of as a dichotomy of "inner" and "outer" realms. To say that mental phenomena are intentional is to say that mental acts can succeed in referring to real, existing objects, so that these acts and their objects cannot be relegated to a domain which is hermetically sealed against an extra-mental or "outer" realm comprising physical phenomena. To deny this dualistic conception of mental and physical phenomena is to avoid the kind of mentalism which, as we have seen, characterises Brentano's original account of the objects to which mental acts are intentionally related.

Behaviourism — one version of which results from the Russell-Quine approach discussed in this chapter — is one way of denying dualism. As the behaviourist sees it, when we consider ourselves to be talking about so-called "mental" states of affairs, processes, etc., we are really talking about quite different states of affairs, *viz.*, physical states of affairs such as dispositions to behave in certain ways (Quine). We might say of the behaviourist, generally, that he denies dualism by attempting to "de-psychologise" the mental. But, behaviourism is not the only way of denying dualism. Implicit in the approach of the "irreducibility theorists" like Chisholm and Anscombe is the view that we can retain the autonomy of the mental without thereby committing ourselves to the kind of dualism which insulates the mental from the "real". Dualism compels us to regard "the real" as the extra-mental. When "the mental" is released from this dualistic setting, there need be no barrier to arguing that mental activities can succeed in referring to the real. In particular, we can show that there is nothing mysterious about "the mental" when we reflect upon the language we use to talk about mental activities. The peculiarities about mental phenomena can be expressed as criteria concerning the logical behaviour of sentences that we use to talk about such phenomena. We might say of such theorists that they deny dualism by attempting to "de-mystify" the mental.

The different approaches to intentionality discussed in these two chapters can now be grouped according to the different ways in which dualism is denied. On the one hand, there are the "irreducibility theorists" like Anscombe and Chisholm, who retain a notion of "the mental" as something which is irreducible but who, by releasing this notion from a dualistic setting, aspire to "de-mystify" it. On the other hand, there are those extensionalists like Russell and Quine, whose orientation is behaviouristic. These philosophers seek to "de-psychologise" the mental; reduce it to the physical.

The specific kind of dualism that is being resisted by the philosophers under discussion is that commonly ascribed to Descartes: a *metaphysical* dualism, turning on the notion of substances which are grasped through their essential attributes, and its accompanying *epistemological* dualism which characterises the mental by privacy and privileged access.[26]

The metaphysical dualism is a dualism of substances. Physical substance is characterised by a hierarchy of predicates (attributes such as "red", "five metres long", etc.) falling under modes (such as colour, dimension, etc.), all of which ultimately presuppose the predicate "is spatially extended". Mental substance is characterised by predicates which do not presuppose extension. The distinction between mental and physical phenomena can thus be stated as a distinction between phenomena characterised by reference to mental predicates as opposed to phenomena characterised by reference to physical predicates.

The accompanying epistemological dualism is a dualism of ways of knowing: Mental phenomena which, for Descartes, are psychological states including sensations such as pain, are known to me directly, that is, non-inferentially and non-observationally. Physical phenomena − that is, states, events and processes in the external world − are known to me only on the basis of observation and inference. Knowledge of the existence and character of such phenomena is always open to the possibility of error. Indubitability, which characterises my knowledge of my own psychological states is absent in the case of my knowledge of the external world and its objects. Mental phenomena are private for they are those phenomena to which I have privileged access.

[26] Whether, in fact, this involves a distortion of Descartes' own views is an interesting question of scholarship in its own right. But it is not immediately relevant to this discussion. For our concern is to identify the kind of dualism and the specific notion of "the mental" that is resisted by these philosophers, rather than to trace the authorship of these ideas or the authenticity of interpretations.

The kind of dualism that is denied by those philosophers under discussion is, then, that Cartesian-derived dualism of mental and physical phenomena in which "the mental" is tied to privacy in this way. To deny dualism is to deny that "the mental" is in any way mysterious: It is to deny that mental activities are to be understood as mysterious operations which perform the "shadow-drama on the ghostly boards of the mental stage",[27] and that the objects of these acts are to be understood as mysterious items in some "mental museum".[28]

The key to the resistance to the Cartesian "mental" here, is the word "mysterious". What makes mental operations and entities mysterious is, in the first instance, the privacy which, on Descartes' account, is tied to mental phenomena: "Human bodies are in space and are subject to mechanical laws which govern all other bodies in space. Bodily processes and states can be inspected by external observers . . . . But minds are not in space, nor are their operations subject to mechanical laws. The workings of one mind are not witnessable by other observers; its career is private . . .".[29]

What makes the Cartesian "mental" something mysterious can't just be privacy, for privacy means privileged access, and hence immediate knowledge or awareness and, therefore, no mystery. What makes the privacy of the mental a source of mystery is this: The mental, if private, is (i) inaccessible to language users (as Wittgenstein's well-known arguments against a private language have shown), and (ii) inaccessible to the scientific procedures of empirical inquiry. (As Ryle and others point out, scientific procedures involve the observation of data. Mental phenomena, if private, are non-observable). If "the mental" is private in either of these senses, then it is mysterious (i) *vis-à-vis* language, and (ii) *vis-à-vis* empirical inquiry.

The first of these leads to the attempt to *retain* "the mental" but to *shed* "the private".[30] This is the way in which the irreducibility theorists attempt to "de-mystify" the mental: The

[27] Ryle (1949), p. 63.

[28] Quine (1968), p. 27.

[29] Ryle (1949), p. 13.

[30] *Cf.* Kenny (1968), pp. 360–1: "If Descartes' innovation was to identify the mental with the private, Wittgenstein's contribution was to separate the two". The irreducibility theorists belong, clearly, to this Wittgensteinian tradition.

mental is characterised by intentionality; intentionality includes the capacity for objective reference; if the mental is characterised by intentionality, then it cannot be necessarily "private". The second of the above considerations leads to the rejection of the mental *along with* privacy. This line of approach is represented by Russell's and Quine's behaviourist theory, which attempts to "de-psychologise" the mental by reducing it to the physical: Mental phenomena have the capacity for objective reference; objective reference is a feature of sentences about physical phenomena; sentences about mental phenomena are, therefore, reducible to sentences about physical phenomena; therefore, "the mental, i.e., private" is a myth and can be dispensed with.

Each of these approaches represents a different way of denying dualism and the characterisation of the mental-as-private which is associated with that dualism. But each of these approaches depends on asserting that the mental has the capacity for objective reference. It is acceptance of this thesis that accounts for the irreducibility theorists' belief that the mental can be retained without the characterisation of privacy. But it is acceptance of this very same thesis, *viz.*, that the mental can achieve objective reference, which leads the relational and behaviourist theorists to reduce the mental to the physical and thereby dispense with both the mental *and* intentionality.

In both of these cases, Cartesian dualism is consciously and deliberately denied. However, although these theories resist dualism, they do exploit *a* distinction of mental and physical phenomena (or psychological vs non-psychological) in the course of arguing their theories. For, as with Brentano, intentionality is what *marks off* the mental from the physical: Intentionality is characteristic of the mental *as contrasted with* the physical. We might say of these philosophers that they make use of a dichotomy of mental and physical (or psychological and non-psychological) while, at the same time, rejecting a *dualistic* conception of the difference. The irreducibility theorists make use of it in order to defend the autonomy of the mental (characterised by intentionality); the relational and behaviourist make use of it in order to repudiate one of the terms of that dichotomy, *viz.*, the mental (and therefore, intentionality).

But it is not clear how one can successfully maintain the claim that a dichotomy of the mental and the physical can be exploited without a commitment to dualism of some kind. For one thing, although Descartes' unsatisfactory notion of "the mental" is dismissed, the contrasting notion of "the physical" (or a version of this) does seem to be retained. In terms of Descartes' dualism, "the physical" is that which is characterised only by physical – i.e., non-mental – predicates. The distinction which is exploited by the philosophers under discussion is one in which "the mental" is alleged to be "de-mystified" or "de-psychologised" but the contrasting notion of "the physical" (or "the non-psychological") is a notion of that which is characterisable without reference to an intentional (i.e., "mental") vocabulary.

I have so far been using the expression "capable of objective reference" in a metaphysically neutral way, that is, without commitment to any theory about what "objectivity of reference" might consist in. We can now see what content is given to this expression by those who (in some sense) accept this as a capacity of the mental. Because all of these philosophers are concerned with *sentences* about the mental (or psychological) the "capacity for objective reference" is to be characterised by appeal to language rather than phenomena.

But it is the language we use to describe *physical* phenomena which provides the paradigm of objective reference. For Russell, "referring to x" is like "kicking x"[31] – there must be some particular x which is kicked. The sentences we use to talk about physical phenomena are extensional, i.e., they both imply existence and admit substitutivity. They are therefore, by Chisholm's criteria, non-intentional. For the relational theorists, it is because these sentences are non-intentional that objective reference is secured. The result of this view, as we have seen, is that those acts – psychological or non-psychological – which are directed to an existing object are described in sentences which are extensional; psychological acts which succeed in achieving reference are non-intentional.

On Anscombe's account, the objective reference which is a possibility for psychological acts means reference to something

[31] This analogy provides a very effective way of stating Russell's view of reference. It was suggested to me, in a different context, by William Godfrey-Smith of the Australian National University.

physical — that is, something which might just as well be the object of a physical act and therefore describable without reference to the psychological or without the use of intentional language. But, as we have seen, for Anscombe the problems arise from an attempt to say that reference to such objects, when they are the objects of *psychological* acts, can be described in sentences which are intentional.

On both of these accounts, intentionality is fundamentally incompatible with objective reference: Objective reference is a feature of the language we use to talk about physical phenomena; because intentionality is what *marks off* sentences about the psychological from sentences about the physical, the latter class of sentences must be non-intentional; objective reference is, therefore, a feature of non-intentional sentences. The incompatibility of intentionality with objective reference is quite explicit in the relational theory, where sentences about psychological acts which succeed in achieving reference are assigned to the category of the non-intentional; the same incompatibility is, however, implicit in Anscombe's account, which attempts to confine such acts to the category of the intentional at the expense of the seemingly intractable puzzles surrounding the notion of objective reference in the case of these acts.

CHAPTER V

SENSE AND THE PSYCHOLOGICAL

§ 1. *Introduction*

When objective reference is characterised relative to a two-levelled semantical framework, serious problems arise for a theory of intentionality. This was particularly evident in Chapter III, where we examined a theory of objective reference based explicitly on Russell's theory of names. At the same time, as we saw at the end of the last chapter, this way of characterising objective reference is one that successfully avoids mentalism and, in this respect, fulfils an important requirement for a theory of intentionality.

The question arises whether this same requirement – the avoidance of mentalism – can also be fulfilled by a theory of intentionality which appeals to Frege's notion of sense. On the negative side, a difficulty is raised by certain contemporary philosophers who accept the Russellian semantical framework. On the one hand, philosophers like Quine (who propose an extensionalist theory of language), and, on the other, philosophers like Kripke and Putnam (who propose a causal theory of names)[1] argue that Fregean sense is tied to a mentalistic theory of meaning. For Quine, intensions (i.e. senses) are what is named by abstract nouns or noun expressions. He argues that a theory of language which admits intensions commits one to the postulation of entities – *viz.*, meanings – which exist in the mind. For the causal theorists, intensions (i.e., senses) are what is grasped in a psychological act. They are said to be constituents of a psychological state. The Fregean thesis that reference is a function of sense is, therefore, interpreted as the thesis that reference is a function of psychological considerations.

[1] Kripke (1972); Putnam (1975).

The charge of mentalism is, therefore, mounted on two levels: For Quine, the intensionalist theory of language entailed by Frege's theory of sense gives rise to ontological mentalism[2] — the postulation of mental entities; for the causal theorists, Frege's theory of sense leads to a psychologistic[3] theory of the determination of reference.

Before we can attempt a defence of Frege, here, we must consider why it is that sense is so readily associated with a mentalistic theory of meaning. It will be useful, at this point, to recall in summary his theory of sense which was discussed in Chapter II, and to state the implications of this theory where the notion of "meaning" is concerned.

1. Every sign necessarily has a sense (meaning) but only contingently a reference;
2. Senses (meanings) are objective in that (i) they are abstract entities, (ii) they are what is grasped by those who speak and understand a common language, (iii) they are possible referents;
3. Sense (meaning) is not the same as reference, for (i) a sign must have a sense, but it need not possess a reference; (ii) different signs with different senses may have the same reference. Where this is so, the signs differ in cognitive value and then cannot, in some contexts, be substituted for one another, *salva veritate*; (iii) the sense is not the reference but the mode in which the reference is presented.
4. Sense (meaning) determines reference.

Frege's theory of sense entails the following:

(I) An intensionalist theory of *language* — that is, one which admits intensional (non-extensional) constructions:[4] An expression

---

[2] *Supra*, Chapter I §1.

[3] *Supra*, pp. 23—25.

[4] It is necessary to re-state, here, the fact that the theory under consideration is one from which Frege's "logical concerns" have been isolated. (*Cf.*, *supra*, pp. 44—46). Included amongst Frege's "logical concerns" is the concern to construct a purely extensional language. Within such a language, there would be a one-one correlation between the sense and reference of each sign — i.e., there would be no instances of different signs with different senses having the same reference. In such a language, the notion of sense would no longer be central. But Frege, in offering us a theory of sense, is offering us a theory from which these concerns have been extracted.

which occurs within an intensional context cannot be replaced by one different in meaning but with the same reference or truth-value without disturbance to the truth-value of the whole sentence (3(ii) above). Frege explains this by saying that, in such contexts, the expression which resists substitutivity refers to a sense (2(iii) above).

(II) A "mind-related" notion of *meaning.* According to 2(ii), meanings — senses — are what is grasped in cognitive activities such as understanding the meaning of *A*, where "*A*" is some expression in a language. Meanings are mind-related in the way that cognitive activities such as understanding or "grasping the meaning of" are mind-related. Understanding cannot just consist in knowing the reference of that term for, by 3(ii), there is a difference in the cognitive value of two expressions with different meanings which refer to the same object. Moreover, by 3(iii), understanding the sense of an expression gives only one-sided "knowledge" of the reference: the sense is a *means* of identifying an object as the referent of that term.

(III) A theory of *reference* as that which is determined by sense: The relation between a sign and its referent is always mediated by sense (4 above). Thus *which* object is a sign's referent — which object is associated with a given sign — is something that is determined by the sense. It is this latter claim which is denied by causal theorists who argue that the fixing of reference in the case of names (including, perhaps, natural kind terms as well) is determined, ultimately, by causal considerations from which "mediation by sense" or by anything "mind-related" is excluded.[5]

For Quine, it is (I) which leads to ontological mentalism: His opposition to Fregean sense is part of his objection to intensionalist theories of language, generally; for the causal theorists, (II) and (III) are seen to lead to a psychologistic theory of reference.

If these objections can be sustained, then our proposed theory of intentionality will involve a circularity: Intentionality of the mental is to be characterised by appeal to Fregean sense; senses are intensions; but intensions are mental entities.

[5] This is not to say that the causal theory is, like Quine's, a theory which makes no appeal to "mind-related" notions, such as speakers' intentions, beliefs, etc. The point is, rather, that none of these things is, at a fundamental level, the *means* by which reference is fixed. See Appendix B.

This seems to leave us with a dilemma: If we abandon the Fregean framework then we fail in our attempt to construct an adequate theory of the intentionality of the mental; alternatively, if we *do* invoke Frege's framework by appealing to his notion of sense, our attempts to characterise intentionality involve a circularity: intentionality remains a mentalistic notion. By way of resolving this dilemma, I shall argue that the second of these claims is to be rejected. This means that Fregean sense must be dissociated from mentalism, specifically from the ontological mentalism alleged by Quine, and from psychologistic theories of the determination of reference as alleged by Putnam.

It is ironic that the charge of psychologism should be levelled against Frege, here, for Frege regarded himself as a vigorous opponent of psychologism, and it was his notions of sense and the thought which he took to be the crucial weapon in his fight against psychologism. For example, in his review of Husserl's early work, *Philosophie der Arithmetik,*[6] Frege was able to show that, without recognition of the distinction between ideas and the thought, Husserl's analysis of arithmetical concepts was irredeemably psychologistic.

Husserl's aim in his *Philosophie der Arithmetik* was to show how the concepts and laws of arithmetic, which have *logical* status, have their origins in subjective *psychological* acts. He believed that Brentano's descriptive method and the theory of presentations, with its dichotomy of act and object,[7] would enable him to carry out this task. He begins with the concept of multiplicity which is presupposed by the concept of number (in the same way that the concept of colour is presupposed by the concept of red). The concept of multiplicity arises from a mental act of collecting objects into a group. This group exists only in virtue of the mental act of referring one term to another and not in virtue of any "internal" relationship depending upon the properties inherent in the objects themselves. This abstract concept of multiplicity, and the arithmetical concepts which are based on this, arise from reflection upon this mental act of collecting objects together. The group has

[6] Husserl (1891).
[7] *Cf. supra*, pp. 24—25. Here, we saw how the theory of presentations with its dichotomy of act and object led, in Brentano's case, to "subjective" psychologism.

objectivity over and above that of its individual members; it can be talked about as a single entity, and, in this respect, is something "other than" its individual members. At the same time, the group as such only exists in virtue of subjective psychological acts. In this way Husserl believed he had established both the objectivity – i.e., the *logical* status – of arithmetical concepts, and, at the same time, the origins of those concepts in subjective *psychological* acts.

However Husserl's theory is based on Brentano's account of presentations with its dichotomy of act and object. If the objects of our acts are presentations, then so too are the concepts which arise from the mental act of collecting those objects together. Presentations are mental occurrences, and, for this reason, a presentation-based account of the concepts of arithmetic can never succeed in establishing the logical status of those concepts.

Frege's way of exposing the psychologism of Husserl's theory[8] was to show that a presentation-based account obscured the important distinctions between ideas and the thought and between the sense and reference of expressions. The first of these distinctions, he claimed, must be observed if we are to establish the logical rather than the psychological status of those concepts, and thereby avoid psychologism. Frege points out that the notion of presentation obscures the distinction between ideas ("the subjective") and the thought ("the objective"):

> For example, one talks of this or that presentation as if, separated from the presentor, it would let itself be observed in public. And yet, no-one has someone else's presentation but only his own, and no-one knows how far his presentation – e.g., that of red – agrees with that of someone else; for the peculiarity of the presentation which I associate with the word 'red', I cannot state (so as to be able to compare it) . . . . With thoughts, it is quite different: one and the same thought can be grasped by many people. The components of a thought, and even more so the things themselves, must be distinguished from the presentations which in the soul accompany the grasping of a thought and which someone has about these things. In combining under the word 'presentation' both what is subjective

[8] Frege (1894).

124

and what is objective, one blurs the boundary between the two in such a way that now a presentation in the proper sense of the word is treated like something objective, and now something objective is treated like a presentation.[9]

The theory of presentations, moreover, obscures the distinction between the sense and reference of expressions − a distinction which, for Frege, must be recognised if we are to explain the identity relation in true statements of the form, $a = b$:[10]

... if words always designated presentations, one could never say, 'A is the same as B'. For to be able to do that, one would already have to distinguish A and B, and then these would simply be different presentations.[11]

In the present chapter, we will see why it is that the notion of sense or the thought, which Frege himself took to be crucial to anti-psychologism, is, in its turn, regarded by some philosophers as a notion tied to a psychologistic theory of reference. The "critique of sense", as it relates specifically to Frege, is an attack on the thesis that meaning − i.e., sense − is mind-related. It is argued by Frege's critics that, if sense is mind-related, then it is a mentalistic notion, in which case we cannot consistently claim that sense is, at

[9] *Ibid*., p. 325. The accuracy of Frege's representation of Husserl, here, has been called into question. Willard (1980) for example, has argued that Frege illegitimately identifies Husserl's presentations with *his* (i.e., Frege's) "ideas". But, nonetheless, he adds, Frege was justified in many of his criticisms: "While Husserl did distinguish the logical from the psychological − indeed, the book in question is divided into its two 'Parts' precisely on the basis of that distinction − he also did not know how to set them clearly into an intelligible relation with one another" (p. 48). Willard's own conclusion is that the psychologism of Husserl's early work resulted from the inadequacy of the concepts borrowed from Brentano's psychology to perform the task undertaken by Husserl.

[10] *Supra*, Chapter II §1.

[11] Frege (1894), p. 327. Frege claims that "psychological logicians" also "lack all understanding of definitions": If words and combinations of words refer to presentations, then for any two of these only two cases are possible: either they designate the same presentation, or they designate different ones. In the first case, equating them by means of a definition is useless, 'an obvious circle'; in the other it is false." (p. 326).

the same time, a vehicle of reference. The difficulty, here, is that Frege offers us no theory of *how* sense is related to the mind. The seriousness of this deficiency becomes apparent in the face of Putnam's critique. In order to meet the kind of objection raised by Putnam, Frege's theory of sense needs to be supplemented by a non-psychologistic theory of the way in which sense or meaning is at once (a) mind-related, and (b) a vehicle of reference. In Chapter VI we will see how Husserl's phenomenological account of linguistic meaning and reference might be invoked to provide this supplementation. I shall turn, now, to the different critiques of sense so that we can specify the kind of mentalism that is imputed to a Fregean-based theory of meaning and reference. For any theory about the relation of meaning and the mind which is invoked to supplement Frege's theory of sense must be one which escapes these criticisms.

§ 2. *Intensions and mental entities*

Sentences which state, in propositional form the content of thought are a sub-class of intensional constructions. The proposition which is the content of thought is, on this analysis, an intensional object — what Frege calls a sense or intension.[12]

Intensions are meanings construed as abstract entities. For Quine, they are the entities named by abstract nouns and noun-expressions. Quine claims that intensions or senses belong to traditional or pre-scientific theories of meaning. These theories of meaning are held to be objectionable because they are *mentalistic.*

Mentalism, according to Quine, is the doctrine which says that (a) meanings are discrete entities, and, (b) these entities exist in the mind.[13] According to mentalistic theories of meaning, meanings are determinate entities, and the words are labels. Quine also speaks of the "idea idea".[14] Meaning is a determinate idea with which a word is associated. From the mentalistic viewpoint, synonymy between different expressions in a language consists in the correspondence of different labels to the same "idea" or

[12] *Supra*, p. 36.
[13] Quine (1968); Quine (1973).
[14] Quine (1973), pp. 34ff.

"meaning entity"; translation from one language to another consists in switching labels — supplying a different expression for the same "idea, thought, meaning, proposition".[15] At the semantical level, "ideas, thoughts, meanings and propositions" are identified with Fregean sense: They are intensional objects, that is to say intensions. Intensions, for Quine, enter into constructions which are opaque, that is, contexts which do not admit quantification, and which are therefore non-truth-functional. Quine says of intensions that they are "creatures of darkness".[16] He says elsewhere that "obscurity is the breeding place of mentalistic semantics".[17] Intensions are, for Quine, a product of mentalistic semantics — they are mental entities. As Quine sees it, intensionalist theories of language commit one to the existence of these "mysterious" entities.

Quine's rejection of mentalism is central to (a) his thesis of the indeterminacy of translation, and (b) his thesis of extensionality. Quine's indeterminacy thesis tells us that rival translations of a native language may be produced, inconsistent with one another, but each compatible with the totality of observed dispositions to verbal behaviour of the native speakers.[18] In this situation there is no question of "the right" translation or of what the natives "really mean". Quine introduces the behavioural notion of "stimulus meaning", which is simply a speaker's dispositions to verbal behaviour, to replace the old mentalistic notion of meaning. For Quine, "Meaning . . . is not a psychic existence; it is primarily a property of behaviour".[19] In giving up the view that meanings are mental entities — what Quine calls "the museum myth", we give up an assurance of determinacy. Quine's indeterminacy thesis, then, involves (i) a denial that there are fixed and determinate meanings; (ii) the claim that meaning is "a property of behaviour", and, therefore, (iii) a denial that meanings are mental entities. It is not always clear whether the inadequacies of mentalistic theories of meaning constitute an argument *for* or a

---

[15] *Ibid.*, p. 36.
[16] Quine (1956), p. 186.
[17] Quine (1968), p. 28.
[18] Quine (1960), pp. 26ff.
[19] Quine (1968), p. 27. See also, p. 29.

consequence *of* Quine's indeterminacy thesis. But clearly, the indeterminacy thesis involves the proposal of a behaviourist theory of "meaning" to replace the old mentalistic theories.

Quine's extensionality thesis tells us (i) that we *can* dispense with the mentalistic notion of meaning that is embodied in the notion of "intension": Intensions enter into constructions which are opaque; sentences which are opaque can be rendered as sentences which are transparent, by manoeuvering the singular term occurring in the opaque context into a position which is "purely referential" (accessible to quantification); in this way intensions are dispensed with, and "meaning" is reduced to the truth-value of the newly-formed extensional sentence. Quine's extensionality thesis — or, at least one aspect of it — tells us, moreover, (ii) that we *must* dispense with the mentalistic notion of meaning. "Meanings", in the mentalistic sense, are "scientifically useless" and, where scientific progress is concerned, they must be abandoned.[20] In terms of the extensionality thesis, the only legitimate notion of meaning is one that is tied to the extensionality of language.

The indeterminacy thesis, therefore tells us that "meaning" is to be re-identified as a property of behaviour rather than as an entity in the mind. "Meaning" is dissociated from "the mind" and is re-located in the physical world, that is to say, in dispositions to verbal behaviour. This revised notion of "meaning" is one that is released from intensionality and is tied instead to the extensionality of language. The extensionality thesis tells us that mentalistic notions are redundant and scientifically useless. Sentences about "the mental" are translatable into

---

[20] Quine (1953a), p. 214; Quine (1960), p. 264—5. Quine is not always consistent on this matter. At times he concedes that it is a matter of choice whether or not we include such entities amongst our ontological commitments: Quine (1950), pp. 77—9; also, Quine (1960), p. 221. However, there is no equivocation on Quine's part about the following: "If we are limning the true and ultimate structure of reality, the canonical scheme for us is the austere scheme which knows no quotation but direct quotation and no propositional attitudes but only the physical constitution and behaviour of organisms." (Quine (1960), p. 221).

sentences about "the physical".[21] As Quine sees it, the behaviourism of the indeterminacy thesis both implies and is implied by the extensionalism of his theory of language.

This theoretical setting provides the context for Quine's claim that (i) intensionalist theories of language admit intensions, and (ii) intensions are mental entities. In order to meet Quine's objections to intensionalist theories of language, we must be able to show either (i) that intensionalism does not (or need not) admit *intensions,* or (ii) that intensions are not *mental* entities.

Arguments for the first of these — for an intensionalism without intensions — are not necessarily arguments in defence of Fregean *sense.* On can accept Frege's principle of non-substitutivity as a principle of language without thereby accepting Frege's *explanation* of that principle, *viz.,* that the words resisting substitutivity refer to a sense. This, in fact, seems to be true of Prior's intensionalism[22] for which the principle of non-substitutivity plays a purely formal role, and the notion of sense plays no role at all. However, for our purposes, it is useful to pay some consideration to Prior's defence of an "intensionalism-without-intensions", for this will serve to demonstrate one way of answering Quine's objection that intensionalist theories of language commit us to introducing mental entities *named by* abstract nouns and noun-expressions.

For Quine, intensionalism is unacceptable for it admits intensions and thereby commits us to the existence of entities named by abstract nouns and noun-expressions. The view that intensionalism means admitting intensions is a consequence of the claim that all variables of quantification are name-variables. That is to say, the grammatical category of expressions they keep place for is that of nouns, and nouns are expressions which stand for some

---

[21] Quine is aware of the kinds of objections raised by Chisholm (*supra,* Chapter IV §1); he actually cites Chisholm's thesis of the irreducibility of intentional idioms as evidence for his indeterminacy thesis. He argues that the irreducibility of intentional idioms is just one of many instances where indeterminacy infects translational synonymy. Whereas Chisholm and the irreducibility theorists take Brentano's thesis as "showing the indispensibility of intentional idioms and the importance of an autonomous science of intention", Quine himself takes that same thesis as "showing the baselessness of intentional idioms and the emptiness of a science of intentions". Quine (1960), pp. 220–1.

[22] Prior (1968); also, Prior (1971), pp. 33–9.

non-linguistic entity. Any object which satisfies a quantified formula is said to be the value of the bound variable(s). The set of objects which constitute the values of the variable is the set of objects to which we are ontologically committed: "To be is to be the value of a variable".[23] If it is only name-variables which are admitted, then we must radically re-word sentences of ordinary language so that the only variables which occur in them are ones that replace grammatical nouns, or, if we are prepared to retain sentences such as "For some ϕ, ϕx" (where the quantified variable replaces an expression of a grammatical category other than noun), then we must nominalise the variable "ϕ", with the unwelcome consequence of admitting into our ontology, "entities" named by e.g., verbs, adjectives, etc. If we admit intensional constructions, such as "A believes that p", then the variable, "p", when bound by a quantifier, will be nominalised thereby committing us to the existence of an entity i.e., an intension, named by the (noun-)expression which "p" holds place for. Because, for Quine, intensions are mental entities, intensional sentences must be radically re-worded so that non-nominal expressions are eliminated from positions accessible to quantification.

Prior argues that (a) we can retain non-nominal variables, that is, variables of a grammatical category other than nouns, and (b) that in so doing, there is no need to treat these variables as if they were names of objects. In the open sentence, "x is red-haired", the variable "x" can be said to take the place of a name, e.g., "Henry", and, in a secondary sense, because names stand for non-linguistic objects or persons, the variable can be said to stand for the person, Henry. In the sentence "Henry ϕ's Tom", the verb-variable, "ϕ's", can be said to stand for – keep the place for – a transitive verb. But it is senseless to ask what it "stands for" in the secondary sense which requires that there be some non-linguistic object for which it stands. Verbs (like adjectives, adverbs etc.) do not have the job of designating entities. Similarly, Prior argues the propositional variable, "p", in "James believes that p" stands for a sentence, but, since it is not the job of sentences to designate objects, there can be no secondary sense in which p can be said to stand for some non-linguistic entity.

[23] Quine (1948).

When these non-nominal variables are bound by a quantifier, they are not thereby nominalised: The sentence, "For some ϕ, Henry ϕ's", is true if some specification of it is true. A specification is simply the replacement of the variable "ϕ" by an expression of the appropriate grammatical kind, *viz.*, a verb-expression. Similarly, "For some p, James believes that p" is true if some specification of it is true. A specification of it is simply the replacement of the variable "p" by an expression of the same grammatical kind, *viz.*, a sentence.

Prior's arguments show us one way of dispensing with entities *named by* abstract nouns without thereby rejecting intensionalism. But the cost of this is the elimination of *intensions*. For Frege, there *are* such entities as intensions, but these entities must be dissociated from Quine's notion of an intension as a "mental entity".

Arguments for intensionalism *with* intensions do not necessarily serve to help us, here. For, where intensionalist theories of language are concerned, the notion of "intension" is a purely formal one. For example, the formal systems of Church and Carnap which admit intensions as values of variables, or those semantic theories which treat intensions as functions across possible worlds, do not have any fundamental bearing on the questions at issue here, *viz.*, questions relating to intensions or senses *qua* entities grasped in acts of understanding. We might say that the notion of "intension" which features in such systems is a notion belonging to Frege's logical concerns — the concerns of formal semantics — and, therefore, a notion which plays no role in a theory of meaning.

Quine, it seems, does not make this separation, and the result is a mis-statement of Frege's position *vis-à-vis* the notion of intension as it relates to Frege's theory of meaning. On Quine's account, Frege's statement that (in intensional contexts) "the words refer to a sense" is taken to mean "the words *name* an entity", where the "naming" is the Russellian notion set against a two-levelled semantical framework. This interpretation is perfectly justified where the notion of "intension" is one relating to the construction of a purely formal language — Frege's logical concerns.[24]

---

[24] This is not to say that there are two notions of "intension" that Frege operates with. As with the notion of reference (*supra*, pp. 44—46), the notion of intension "behaves" differently according to whether we see it in terms of a two- or three-levelled framework.

Within the two-levelled framework, there are only signs and referents (for Quine, the entities to which we are ontologically committed; for Russell, the objects with which we are acquainted); what is *referred to* by words occurring in an intensional context must, in terms of this framework, be regarded as entities alongside material objects, etc., which are the customary referents of most names.

But, as we have already seen, the setting for Frege's theory of meaning is a three-levelled semantical framework. If the notion of intension which enters into Frege's theory of meaning is characterised relative to a two-levelled framework, the result is, inevitably, a misrepresentation of Frege's position.[25] For, if we agree that intensions are *entities named*, in a sense relative to the two-levelled framework, then these entities will belong to what Frege calls "the realm of things". And yet, for Frege, intensions or thoughts "are not wholly unactual but their actuality is quite different from the actuality of things".[26] They belong to the "third realm". Because the constraints of a two-levelled framework do not admit a distinction of sense and reference, no "third realm" — the realm of thoughts or senses which can be referred to — can be recognised.

But the inadequacies of characterising intensions by appeal to a two-levelled framework, here, can be demonstrated without appeal to Frege's ontology. On Quine's account, intensions or meanings are said to be mental entities or ideas. For Frege, quite explicitly, intensions, that is, thoughts, are public and shareable and must therefore be distinguished from ideas which are private and non-shareable. The distinctions necessary for our understanding of Frege's "intensions" here — *viz.*, between sense and reference, and between ideas and thoughts — are not available to one who is operating within a two-levelled semantical framework; consequently, any notion of "intension" which introduces such a framework will not be the notion of intension or the thought which relates to Frege's theory of meaning.

Fregean sense can be defended against the kinds of objections

[25] The mis-statement of Frege's position, here, is analogous to Russell's misrepresentation of Fregean sense which results from the attempt to accommodate *a* notion of "sense" within a two-levelled framework. See Appendix A.

[26] Frege (1918), p. 29.

arising from Quine's philosophy, simply by demonstrating that it is not the notion of intension relating to Frege's theory of meaning that is under criticism in his theory. A more serious challenge to Fregean sense, however, is that posed by the causal theorists to whom we now turn. Here, we find that, although there seems to be no *prima facie* misrepresentation of Frege's notion of sense, the thesis that sense is "mind-related" is interpreted to mean that sense is tied to a psychologistic theory of the determination of reference. I now turn to these criticisms.

§3. *Sense and psychologism*

The second line of criticism directed to Fregean sense is initiated by the causal theorists. Here, the main target of the attack is Frege's thesis that reference is a function of sense. Because sense is "mind-related", this thesis is held to be an instance of the view shared by "traditional" philosophers, *viz.*, that reference is a function of psychological considerations — knowledge, beliefs, intentions, etc. Theories which view reference this way are said to be psychologistic theories of reference.

At a general level, it seems to be *Russell's* epistemologically-based theory of reference which is taken as the model for such theories. At this level, the Fregean thesis that reference is a function of sense is identified with the Russellian thesis that reference is a function of acquaintance, and by virtue of this identification, is discredited as a psychologistic theory of reference. Criticisms of Fregean sense are advanced at a more specific level however, by Putman, and it is here that we are able to see why sense is taken to be a psychologistic notion and why it is that sense is linked with the Russellian epistemology. After a brief consideration of the more general critique of psychologistic theories of reference, I shall turn to Putnam's explicit criticisms of Fregean sense.

Proponents of the causal theory of names retain the Russellian two-levelled semantical framework, but claim to dispense with the epistemological presuppositions on which Russell's own theory of reference is based. Names necessarily refer, but, for the causal theorists, this is a metaphysically-based necessity, rather than an epistemological one.[27] Moreover, the Russellian distinction

[27] *Supra*, p. 60.

between names and descriptions is retained but, again, for the causal theorists, this distinction turns on the logical features of names rather than on epistemological considerations relating to the corrigibly and the incorrigibly known.

There is both a positive and a negative aspect to the causal theory of names. The positive thesis which states that reference, in the case of a name, is a causally-based relation, is not of immediate concern to us here.[28] It is, rather, one of the negative theses which is important to us – *viz.*, the critique of those theories which hold that *reference is a function of psychological considerations* (knowledge, beliefs, intentions, "information", etc.). Russell is seen to be a main protagonist of this kind of theory, for his Cartesian-derived epistemology leads inevitably to a psychologistic theory of reference: Reference, in the case of a genuine name, is, for Russell, *a function of our acquaintance* with some object; reference, therefore depends not just upon the existence of the object referred to, but on our infallible knowledge of that thing's existence. Russell's theory of reference might, therefore, justifiably be called a psychologistic theory of reference,[29] insofar as any account of the determination of a name's reference will be, ultimately, a psychological account – *viz.*, one in which a description of *what* is referred to by a name involves a description of a psychological state or process – in this case, our acquaintance with what is referred to.[30]

Frege's thesis that *reference is a function of sense* is equated with this discredited Russellian thesis, *viz.*, that reference is determined by psychological considerations. A justification for equating Frege's thesis with psychologistic theories generally,

---

[28] See Appendix B.

[29] *Supra*, pp. 51ff.

[30] There is a corollary to this theory about reference in the case of names: Because, in the case of ordinary proper names, the reference is not something known by acquaintance, these "names" are, for Russell, really disguised descriptions whose reference is known only corrigibly. This aspect of Russell's account of names might provide grounds for including this theory amongst "description theories" of names, these being theories which are also under criticism by the causal theorists. With *this* move, Russell's account of names as disguised descriptions would come to be identified with *Frege's* thesis that every name has a sense, where the latter is taken to be a paradigm case of a "description theory" of reference. See Appendix B.

and with Russell's in particular, is provided by Putnam.[31] Putnam's critique of Fregean sense is presented in the context of Putnam's own version of the causal theory. On this version, the causal doctrine is extended to natural kind terms such as "water", "gold", etc. Putnam argues that the extension of such terms is fixed, not by psychological considerations, but by causal ones.[32] The theories under criticism here are those which equate meaning with intension or concept (in the case of a natural kind term) or with sense (in the case of a name). Intensions, senses and concepts[33] are said to be notions tied to traditional, "mentalistic" theorists of meaning, and Frege's account of sense and reference is seen to be representative of such theories. Putnam says of such theories that (a) they involve an unwarranted *idealisation* of meaning; (b) they assume that meaning is a function of a *psychological state*; and (c) they entail a psychologistic theory of the determination of a term's *reference* or extension.

According to Putnam, the equation of meaning with a term's intension implies an unwarranted idealisation of "meaning" – *viz.*, that a "meaning" is a discrete entity associated with a word. This idealisation is, in part, the result of one way of dissolving an ambiguity surrounding the locution, "what some term, *X*, *means*".[34] The verb "means" here can sometimes be taken to mean "has as extension"; sometimes it is taken in such a way that the expression as a whole means "the intension of *X*". The nominalisation, "meaning", can never mean extension. Therefore, the idealisation of "meaning" involves both the claim that meanings are *entities*, and, at the same time, an insistence that

---

[31] Putnam (1975).

[32] This is not to say that, for Putnam (or for any of the causal theorists), "psychological" considerations are irrelevant to the fixing of a term's reference. It means rather that, for these theorists, reference in the case of genuine naming expressions (which, for Putnam includes natural kind terms), is ultimately a causally-based notion rather than a "psychologically"-based one.

[33] Putnam chooses as his example of a mentalistic notion of meaning the notion of a term's "intension". This he takes to be at once, (a) a sense or concept associated with a term, and (b) the set of necessary and sufficient conditions for something's being a member of the extension of that term. He aims to show that "intension", in either of these senses, is a mentalistic notion.

[34] Putnam (1975), pp. 217; 224.

"meaning" = *intension,* never extension. Two terms may have the same extension, but differ in intension, as in "creature with a heart" and "creature with a kidney". We say that the two expressions have different meanings. Here, meaning = intension. The meaning (i.e., intension) of a term is the concept associated with that term. Concepts are mental. Therefore, meanings are *mental* entities.

Putnam concedes that philosophers like Frege and Carnap regarded concepts or meanings as abstract entities. However, "'grasping' these abstract entities was still an individual psychological act".[35] He adds: "None of these philosophers doubted that understanding a word (knowing its intension) was just a matter of being in a certain psychological state".[36]

In a general sense, a psychological state is, for Putnam, a state which is studied or described by psychology. In the more specific sense, it is a state which assumes the principle of "methodological solipsism": "This assumption is the assumption that no psychological state, properly so-called, presupposes the existence of any individual other than the subject to whom the state is ascribed".[37] A psychological state is not necessarily private. Different people may be said to be in the same psychological state. For example, "knowing that I is the meaning of A", where "I" is an intension and "A" is a term, is the same psychological state for whoever happens to be in it. According to Putnam, traditional theories imply the claim that "knowing the meaning of A", where "A" is a term, is a matter of "knowing that some intension, I, is the meaning of A"; if "I_1" and "I_2" are different intensions and "A" is a term, then "knowing that I_1 is the intension of A" is a different psychological state from "knowing that I_2 is the intension of A".

We can summarise the theory of meaning imputed to traditional theorists represented by Frege as follows: Meanings are said to be entities; they are the entities which are grasped in psychological acts; *knowing the meaning of a term is "just a matter of being in a psychological state".*[38] This last statement is said to be an

[35] *Ibid.,* p. 218.
[36] *Ibid.*
[37] *Ibid.,* p. 220.
[38] *Ibid.,* p. 219.

"unwarranted assumption"[39] on which traditional, mentalistic theories of meaning are based.

The thesis that (a) knowing the meaning of an expression (i.e., knowing its intension or grasping its sense) is just a matter of being in a psychological state, together with the thesis that (b) meaning determines reference, jointly entail a psychologistic theory of the determination of reference: Reference is a function of meaning; meaning is a "constituent" of a psychological state, in the sense that any account of meaning involves reference to the psychological state of "knowing that . . . is the meaning of . . .", reference is, therefore, determined by psychological considerations.

§4. *Varieties of mentalism*

We are now in a position to specify the content of the different kinds of mentalistic theories imputed to Frege. To assist us in this, let us introduce two protagonists of mentalistic theories of meaning: Mr. Antiquine defends the kind of mentalism objected to by Quine – the antithesis of Quine's own theory; Mr. Antiput defends the specific mentalistic doctrine which Putnam finds offensive, and which is seen to be the antithesis of a causal theory of reference.

Mr. Antiquine's position is quite simple-minded. He asserts that meanings are determinate entities and that these entities exist in

[39] The second of the "unwarranted assumptions" on which traditional mentalistic theories of meaning are based is said to be the thesis that "intension determines extension". To equate this with Frege's thesis that "sense determines reference" would involve a serious over-simplification. For, although Putnam is justified in treating the Fregean notions of "sense", "intensions" and "concepts" interchangeably, insofar as these are all said to be grasped in acts of understanding the meaning of a term, there can be no justification for using the notions of "reference" and "extension" interchangeably. For Frege, the reference (*Bedeutung*) of a predicative expression is a concept; the extension of a term, on the other hand, is generally taken to mean the set of objects of which that term is true. It is not clear, however, that Putnam *is* imputing this second "unwarranted assumption" to Frege, so we will not be pursuing this question. His general arguments to show that "sense", "intension", etc., are "psychological" notions are (if successful) sufficient to show how the "authentic" Fregean thesis, *viz.*, that sense determines reference, might be regarded as a psychologistic thesis.

the mind of a speaker. The identity of these entities is known either through introspection or else it is inferred through the behaviour of the speaker. They are the "ideas", "images" or "thoughts" behind the words. On the question of whether they are private, in the sense of being possessable only by a single individual, he equivocates: He insists, on the one hand, that they are inaccessible to public scrutiny — they are not observable because they are something other than, and in addition to, items of behaviour. They are "private" in the sense that they are non-observable. On the other hand, he wants to explain linguistic communication in terms of attaching words or sentences to "the same meaning". And, moreover, he wants to say that translation from one language to another consists in switching the labels of the single identical entity which is the *"real* meaning". This suggests that these entities are somehow shared or common to the minds of language-users. Perhaps the introduction of the principle of methodological solipsism would enable Mr. Antiquine to maintain simultaneously that these mental entities were both private, that is non-observable, and shareable by common speakers of a language.

Mr. Antiput shares the view that meanings are mental entities. But his position is more sophisticated than that of Mr. Antiquine. For his mentalism is at once a *consequence* of (a) his thesis that meaning is a function of psychological state, and also *the grounds for* (b) his thesis that reference is determined by psychological considerations.

To understand the meaning of some term, A, is to be in a particular psychological state. What makes "the meaning of A" a mental entity, here, is the fact that it cannot be specified without reference to the psychological act of understanding or grasping it. The psychological state comprises both the psychological act (of understanding) and the content of the act — what is grasped or understood, i.e., "the meaning". Thus Mr. Antiput can argue that even if it is asserted that concepts, for example, are Platonic entities or abstract objects, *because* they are tied to an individual psychological act in this way they are constituents of a describable psychological state and have therefore merely psychological status. It is the assumption of methodological solipsism which "guarantees" that the contents of such acts have psychological status. The "meaning" which is grasped in an act of understanding has no status independently of that psychological act. To say that the content of this act necessarily has psychological status need not mean that such acts and their contents are private. If understanding the meaning of *A* is describable as a psychological state, then the principle of methodological solipsism does not prevent us from saying that other people can be in *the same* psychological state. But nonetheless, on this view, meaning is *mind-dependent.*

Reconstructed in this way, Mr. Antiput's theory can be identified as a psychologistic theory of meaning. Meaning — what is grasped in a psychological act of understanding — has merely psychological status. Inquiries concerning meanings or concepts are, at a fundamental level, inquiries into psychological states.

But it is precisely these two psychologistic features of Mr. Antiput's theory which are, for Putnam, the characteristics of *Frege's* theory of meaning: Mr. Antiput can acknowledge Frege's resistance to treating concepts as mental *particulars* (by continuing to admit them as abstract or Platonic entities), and yet still argue that they are "mental entities" in the broader sense of having psychological status: "For even if meanings are 'Platonic' entities rather than 'mental' entities ..., 'grasping' those entities is presumably a psychological state".[40] Furthermore, Mr. Antiput can recognise the "public" aspect of meaning insisted on by Frege by allowing that different people may be said to be in *the same* psychological state.

We distinguished earlier two forms of psychologism:[41] reductive psychologism — according to which necessary truths were reduced to empirical generalisations about mental processes, and subjective psychologism — according to which necessary truths were held to be immanent to the act which grasped them. As with reductive psychologism, Mr. Antiput's theory can secure the "public" aspect of the content of thought — in this case, the meaning of a term — but, as with all forms of psychologism, his theory is unable to assert the independent status of *what* is grasped in an act of understanding. *What* is grasped has only psychological status — it is part of a particular, though shareable, psychological state, and belongs therefore to the domain of psychology.

[40] *Ibid.*, p. 222.
[41] *Supra*, pp. 24–25.

Mr. Antiput's second thesis — concerning the determination of reference — is premissed on this psychologistic theory of meaning. True to Frege, he believes that meaning determines reference. Meaning is in turn determined by psychological state. Therefore reference is determined by "psychological considerations". We can moreover specify what these "psychological considerations" are. "Understanding the meaning of A" is equated with the psychological state of "*knowing* that I is the meaning of A". The psychological state here is one which involves an epistemological relation. Therefore, if reference is determined by meaning, then reference is an *epistemologically-based* relation. At this point Mr. Antiput begins to look like a badly-disguised Lord Russell, for whom reference, in the case of a name, is ultimately a matter of a special kind of knowledge — i.e., acquaintance.

Thus Mr. Antiput's mentalism consists in

(a) a form of psychologism, according to which meanings which are grasped in an act of understanding (i.e., the contents of psychological acts) are said to have merely psychological status; and

(b) an epistemologically-based notion of reference, according to which reference is a function of the psychological state of knowing what some term means.

For Putnam, Frege is specifically identified with the first of these, Russell with the second — the Fregean doctrine of sense and the Russellian doctrine of acquaintance are alike tarred with the "mentalistic" brush. Putnam's critique is a direct denial of two important theses which we have been defending: He denies

(i) that Frege's "thought" is objective — i.e., does not have mere psychological status, and

(ii) that there is a significant difference between the Fregean and the Russellian theories of the determination of reference.

The fact that Putnam is able to deny each of these claims is, in fact, due to a deficiency in Frege's theory of sense. Frege's theory tells us *that* thoughts are objective, and *that* thoughts are what is grasped in understanding. But he provides no theory of *how* sense or the thought can be both of these things. He offers no account of the way in which sense or the thought relates to the mind. His theory of sense is therefore susceptible to the interpretations discussed above which so readily equate the "mind-relatedness" of sense with a mentalistic notion of meaning.

It will be argued in the next chapter that if the "mind-relatedness" of sense is explained in terms of an intentional theory of the relationship between meaning and the mind, then the charge of psychologism can be avoided. If sense is taken to be an *intentional* notion, then we can show that sense or the thought is at once mind-related *and* objective. Moreover, if sense is taken to be an intentional notion, then Frege's account of the determination of reference can be successfully dissociated from Russell's epistemologically-based account. For Russell's epistemological relation of direct acquaintance is a paradigm case of a *non-intentional* relation.

CHAPTER VI

INTENTIONALITY: THE VEHICLE OF
OBJECTIVE REFERENCE

§ 1. *Introduction*

Our deliberations in Chapter V have underlined the need to show *how* sense can be at once (a) mind-related, and (b) a vehicle of reference. Frege's thesis that reference is mediated by sense is threatened if the "mind-relatedness" of sense is explained ultimately by appeal to a psychologistic theory of meaning.

What we require, then, is a non-psychologistic theory of the way in which meaning relates to the mind. Frege tells us *that* meaning is *what* is grasped in an act of understanding, and moreover that meaning is what is grasped *in common* by those who communicate a language. But Frege does not give us a theory about the relationship between the cognitive act and its (public, shareable) content.

If Husserl's philosophy is to provide the necessary supplementation for Frege's theory of sense, then there are two requirements that must be met:
(i) his theory must incorporate Frege's notion of sense, and therewith Fregean three-levelled semantical framework;
(ii) his theory must be a non-psychologistic one.

§ 2. *Husserl's theory of intentionality: the Fregean connection*

Husserl's theory of intentionality is a theory about acts of consciousness. Consciousness consists in acts[1] of intending some

---

[1] The ascription of intentionality to *acts* of consciousness is clearly derived from Brentano. However, the replacement of Brentano's "presentations" by "consciousness" as the bearer of intentionality signals Husserl's departure from Brentano's psychologism. For presentations are always immanently directed acts; objects of consciousness, however, are in general "transcendent" to the individual act. Husserl's theory of intentionality is developed primarily in relation to the latter transcendently directed acts, exemplified by perception.

object. Perceiving, imagining, wishing for, thinking of, are different ways of intending some object — they are all *intentional*
acts. To say that consciousness is intentional is to say that all
consciousness is consciousness *of* something.[2] But the object *to*
which the act is directed — the "intended object" — may or may
not exist. Therefore it cannot be the existence of the intended
object which constitutes the intentionality of the act. The intentionality of consciousness consists rather in the fact that to every
act, there is correlated a *noema* or meaning through which the act
is *directed* to its object, if it has one.[3] "To be *directed* simply is to
have a noema".[4]

All consciousness, then, is to be understood in terms of an act
of *A*'s intending some object, *B*. Perceiving, imagining, thinking of,
etc., are all instances of such an act. The intentionality of the
relation between an act and its object in *A*'s intending *B* is to be
understood in terms of the trichotomy:

act — *noema* (meaning) — object.

This trichotomy replaces Brentano's dichotomy of

act — object,[5]

as the framework for elucidating the notion of intentionality.

[2] Here again we see Brentano's direct influence on Husserl. However, for
Husserl, intentionality consists in the *directedness* of acts, rather than in the
correlation with an *object*.

[3] We must be careful to distinguish between: (i) "the object *which is*
intended"; "the object *to* which the act is directed"; "intended object"; and
(ii) "the object *as* intended"; "the intended (perceived, remembered, etc.,) *as*
such". The phrase "intentional object", as we have been using it so far, is
ambiguous as to these two uses. I shall, therefore, avoid using it in connection
with Husserl. Instead, I shall in general use "intended object" to cover the
uses of the expressions in (i), and "noema" to cover those in (ii).

[4] Føllesdal (1972), p. 422.

[5] *Cf. ibid.*, p. 421–2. Here we see, in Husserl's post-psychologistic thought,
a recognition that we need to replace a two-levelled framework by a three-
levelled one, if psychologism is to be avoided. This, of course, was Frege's
essential insight in his scathing review of Husserl's earlier psychologistic
work. (Frege (1894)). The question of whether Husserl's conversion to anti-
psychologism was the direct result of Frege's critique is a subject of continuing debate (see Føllesdal (1958); Mohanty (1974); Willard (1980)), but it
is not of immediate concern here.

Husserl says that "the noema is nothing but a generalisation of the idea of meaning to the field of all acts".[6] This statement is the basis for Føllesdal's authoritative and scholarly exposition of Husserl's notion of noema in terms of the notion of *Sinn* — specifically, Frege's notion of *Sinn*.[7] Føllesdal's exposition of Husserl's notion of noema contains twelve theses, each of which provides the justification for explicating the notion of noema by appeal to Fregean *Sinn*. The first of these states that the noema is an intensional entity, a generalisation of meaning (Føllesdal's Thesis 1). Føllesdal points out that the noema has two components: (i) the "noematic *Sinn*" which is common to all acts which have the same object given in the same manner regardless of the "thetic" character of the act (i.e., of whether they are acts of perceiving, imagining, etc.), and (ii) the "noematic correlate" which differs in acts of different thetic character (Føllesdal's Thesis 2).

We can now summarise Føllesdal's exposition of noema in terms of *Sinn*, by stating Frege's theses concerning sense and matching the Husserlian theses against these. (Føllesdal's theses are enumerated in parentheses):

1. Every sign necessarily has a sense but only contingently a reference.

1′. To each act, there is correlated a noema (Thesis 7), although there need not exist an object.

2. Senses are objective: they are abstract entities or thoughts which belong (ontologically) to the "third realm"; they are possible referents; they are what is grasped in the understanding and communication of a language.

2′. Noemata are abstract entities (Thesis 8) and are, therefore, not perceivable through the senses (Thesis 9). In this respect, noemata are comparable to Frege's "thoughts" which, although ontologically independent of mere ideas, are still not to be located in the realm of material perceptible objects. Noemata can be known through a special act of phenomenological reflection (Thesis 10) and this reflection can be iterated — the noema of an act can be made an object of a further act of reflection (Thesis 11). This tells us that noemata, like Fregean senses, are possible referents. Noemata are the referents of a

---

[6] *Ibid.*, p. 422. *Cf.* Husserl (1913), pp. 257–267.
[7] Føllesdal (1969).

special phenomenological act. Finally, noemata — or, more specifically, the noematic *Sinn* (Thesis 2) — is what is common to many acts which intend the same object in the same manner. In this sense, the noematic *Sinn* is the shared component in acts directed to the same object.

3. Sense is not the same thing as reference.

3'. The noema is not the same thing as the object of an act (Thesis 4): Different noemata may correspond with the same object (Thesis 6) just as different senses may be correlated with the same referent. Just as for Frege, sense is "a mode of presentation" of the object rather than the object itself, so for Husserl, noemata are the modes under which an object is given to different perspectives: The identical object may be intended from a variety of different perspectives, and this means that the identical object is intended throught different noemata (Thesis 12).

4. Sense is the means by which reference is determined.

4'. Acts which are correlated with the same noematic *Sinn* intend the same object although the converse does not hold (the same object may be correlated with *different* noematic *Sinne*). The object is therefore a function of the noematic *Sinn* (Thesis 5). The noematic *Sinn* is the means by which consciousness relates to an object (Thesis 3). The noema is a complex system of determinations (Thesis 12). The object is therefore "transcendent" insofar as it is "intendable" under a multiplicity of perspectives, none of which, individually, "exhausts" the object.

In recent studies of Husserl's phenomenology, we find that Føllesdal's fundamental thesis of explicating Husserl's "noema" by appeal to Fregean sense has been extended and elaborated in some very valuable ways. For example, it has been argued convincingly that Husserl's "noemata" are the very same entities as Frege's intensional objects or intensions, and that Husserl's "transcendent object" — the object *which is* intended or *to* which the act is directed — can be identified with Frege's referent.[8] The identification of noema with meaning or *Sinn* has prompted the suggestion

---

[8] *Cf.* McIntyre & Smith (1971), (1975). Also Aquila (1974); Küng (1972), (1973), (1975); Hintikka (1976).

that Husserl's theory of the intentionality of consciousness is to be understood on the model of a semantic relation;[9] because noema is equated with *Fregean Sinn*, we can justifiably expect it to be Frege's theory of sense and reference which provides the appropriate semantic model.

It is generally believed by those undertaking these explorations that the ideas of Frege and Husserl are mutually illuminating. My own explorations, in the following pages, will be directed primarily towards showing how Husserl's theory of intentionality and his phenomenological approach to linguistic meaning and reference can assist us in overcoming some of the difficulties which arise from the Fregean semantic model.

Føllesdal's fundamental insight was to demonstrate how Husserl and Frege share a three-levelled framework -- Husserl's trichotomy of

act -- noema -- object

being a parallel of Frege's trichotomy of

sign -- sense -- reference.

Because noema = Fregean sense, we can say that Husserl shares Frege's three-levelled *semantical* framework. Husserl's distinction of act, noema and object, however, is the result of a phenomenological approach to the intentionality of consciousness. Frege's distinction of sign, sense, referent belongs to a non-phenomenological theory of linguistic meaning and reference. Our first task, then, is to show what is distinctive about a "phenomenological approach" and to show how it is that this approach can yield distinctions which are compatible with those drawn by Frege. We can then see how a phenomenological account of the intentionality of acts might be invoked to supplement Frege's theory of sense.

Phenomenology is the description of the structures of intentionality. This, as we will see, means a description of noematic structures. A phenomenological description of acts of consciousness is undertaken from a particular standpoint, *viz.*, the

[9] Olafson (1975).

perspective of the experiencing subject.[10] This means that the description of acts of consciousness must be free of any presuppositions which appeal to "transcendent realities": A phenomenological description cannot presuppose any metaphysical theories concerning e.g. the reality of the object intended in an act. Nor can it presuppose any distinctions which are postulated "from outside" the phenomenological standpoint. Phenomenologically, intentionality cannot be seen as a feature which *marks off* the mental from the physical. For a distinction between mental and physical phenomena can only be drawn *on the basis of* our description of the intentionality of acts of consciousness.[11] If phenomenology is to be presuppositionless, then our description of acts of consciousness cannot presuppose either the existence or the non-existence of the object to which the act is directed (the "intended object").

The insistence that phenomenology be "presuppositionless" is Husserl's way of severing phenomenology from the empirical or descriptive sciences.[12] In *Ideas,* Husserl's phenomenology of perception,[13] Husserl makes this point by introducing the controversial notion of the *epoché*. The *epoché* is a methodological device whereby we suspend or bracket questions concerning the existence or non-existence of a spatio-temporal "fact-world". Such questions belong to the "thesis of the natural attitude". The natural attitude is that adopted (quite legitimately) by natural or

[10] *Cf.* Brentano's descriptive psychology discussed *supra*, pp. 19ff. Husserl originally called his phenomenology a "descriptive psychology", but abandoned this title to emphasise the fact that phenomenology is not a branch of the natural sciences, nor is it to be identified with Brentano's descriptive psychology. This terminological revision is significant in the second edition (1913) of the *Logical Investigations*. It is J.N. Findlay's translation of this second edition which forms the basis of the discussion of the work in the present chapter.

[11] In respect of this point, we can see why Brentano's approach is non-phenomenological: Brentano's theory presupposes a distinction between mental phenomena in terms of the objects of inner and outer perception. It is *against this setting* that Brentano hopes to state the descriptive features which are unique to mental phenomena, i.e., the objects of inner perception.

[12] Husserl's abandonment of the title, "descriptive psychology", might well be seen as linked with this intent.

[13] Husserl (1913).

empirical scientists.[14] This perspective embodies certain assumptions — for example, that there exists a world independently of my experiencing it, that this world consists of objects which conform to causal laws, that these facts and laws pertaining to the external world are "given". Most importantly, the natural standpoint involves a "naturalising" of consciousness: consciousness is regarded as a process or state, existing in time (and, perhaps in space as well) along with other events and states of affairs.[15] In performing the *epoché*, we bracket or disconnect the thesis of the natural attitude. The result is a shift in attitude — a shift to the phenomenological attitude towards consciousness and its objects.

The problems surrounding the *epoché* — and these are usually seen to be the practical problems in implementing the *epoché* — do not immediately concern us here. Its relevance to our present concerns is as follows: (a) the deployment of the *epoché* is consistent with what Husserl means by a "presuppositionless" approach to consciousness; (b) the notion of the *epoché* can be seen as an artificial way of stressing that the truth of an intentional statement and therefore the analysis of an intentional act — *A* intends *B* — does not imply or presuppose the existence or non-existence of the intended object (just as "*A* intends *p*" does not imply or presuppose any fact such as the truth of "*p*"), and (c) it is Husserl's way of distancing phenomenology from those empirical sciences which seek to describe (and theorise about) consciousness and its objects as "real" events located in the spatio-temporal "fact-world".

What remains after the thesis of the natural attitude has been suspended is the intentionality of consciousness: the fact that *to every conscious act (noesis) there corresponds a noema*. The *epoché*, as it were, "clears the way" so that the noematic structures or meanings, rather than the intended object, become the focus of our investigation. So, when Husserl says that by means of the *epoché* we effect a change in attitude, he does not mean a change of attitude to the object of consciousness somehow "stripped of its existence".[16] It is not an attitude to the object at all, but a

---

[14] *Ibid.*, pp. 101–3; 105–6.
[15] Husserl (1911), pp. 79ff.
[16] McIntyre & Smith (1971), p. 558; *cf.* Küng (1975).

focussing on the noematic structures of acts of consciousness. At the same time, however, the noema is the means by which consciousness relates to its object, when there is one. So an investigation of, for example, the perceptual noema will be a description of the perceived object *as perceived.* This may be illuminated by means of a familiar example — that of my perceiving a tree.

A phenomenological account of my perceiving a tree will distinguish between the act of perceiving, the object *which* is intended in that act, and the perceived *as such* (the object *as* intended). In perceiving a tree, I perceive only one aspect of the object and then maybe only indeterminately as a greenish object. This single act of perception carries certain expectations — for example, that the tree has a back and sides not available to the present act of perception. But these expectations are "fulfillable" in further perceptual acts as when I walk around the tree and perceive it from different angles, when I touch it, perhaps count the leaves, and so forth. The noema of the initial single act of perception — the perceived as such — points to or "refers itself to" further perceptual acts which may or may not fulfil the initial expectations. If, in performing these further perceptual acts I find that, for example, the tree has no back or sides — that it is a cardboard facsimile, or even perhaps that it is an hallucination — then my pattern of expectations is frustrated: the noema of my act then becomes a different one with a different pattern of expectations.

The expectations carried by the noema are not always determinate — we may, for example, expect to find certain colours on the hidden sides of a tree but we may not be sure what colours we will find. Or we may expect that there will be leaves on the other side, but unsure as to how many. Successive perceptual acts, while fulfilling certain determinate expectations, will at the same time make determinate many of those expectations which were previously left open. Our experience of the tree throughout these acts becomes richer. At the same time, however, there will be infinitely many expectations which are left indeterminate or unfulfilled. The object is "inexhaustible" or *transcendent.*[17] To say that the intended object is transcendent is not to say that what we experience (the perceived as such) is something other than the object

[17] Husserl (1913), pp. 130ff.

itself (the object which is perceived), in the way in which some have held that the sense-impressions which we experience are something different from the thing itself — the cause of those impressions. What we experience *is* the object but under different modes or from different perspectives. To say that the intended object is transcendent means that (i) the same identical object — the object which is perceived — is susceptible to a variety of modes of presentation; (ii) that the object, which is given perspectivally, cannot be identified with what is given in a particular perspective; (iii) that no single act of perceiving "exhausts" the object — there are always further possible acts of intending that object.

If perceiving were non-perspectival, then the object perceived would be wholly present in the particular perceptual act. It would come into being and cease to be with the performance of that act. Such an item would be "immanent" to the act.[18] "The inability to be perceived immanently . . . belongs in essence . . . to the thing as such, to every reality . . . Thus the Thing itself, *simpliciter*, we call transcendent".[19] The object *which is* perceived is that which can *only* appear (is only perceivable) perspectivally: "Spatial Being . . . can 'appear' only with a certain 'orientation', which necessarily carries with it sketched out in advance the system of arrangements which makes fresh orientations possible, each of which again corresponds to a certain 'way of appearing', which we perhaps express as a being presented from this or that 'aspect' and so forth".[20] Correlatively, we can say of an act of perceiving that the "possibility of passing over into determinate, ordered, continuous perceptual patterns, which can always be continued, and are therefore never exhausted",[21] belongs to the very structure of the act. Perception is "the consciousness of a *single* perceptual thing

---

[18] Husserl's distinction between "immanently directed" and "transcendently directed" acts replaces Brentano's distinction between "inner" and "outer" perception. He says that there are "serious objections" (*Ibid.*, p. 124) to the latter way of speaking. The objections are, of course, to the distinction of mental and physical phenomena *presupposed by* this manner of speaking.

[19] *Ibid.*, pp. 133–4.

[20] *Ibid.*, pp. 134–5.

[21] *Ibid.*, p. 135.

appearing with ever-increasing completeness, from endlessly new points of view, and with ever-richer determinations".[22]

Husserl's theory of the intentionality of perception enables us to see how certain of the puzzles that plagued Anscombe's account of perception[23] might be avoided. Husserl's intended object — the object *which is* perceived — is transcendent and, therefore, not something which can be given under all its determinations in a single act of perceiving. Thus, like Anscombe's "material object", it is describable independently of any single act of perceiving it. But, on the other hand, a description of the perceived *as such* — what, for Anscombe, is the "intentional object" — is a description of the noema, that is, of the mode in which the object is intended. At a superficial level, Husserl's "noema" is analogous to Anscombe's "intentional object", which she says is characterised by possible non-existence, possible indeterminacy and, in the case of descriptions of the object, failure of substitutivity. In the case of the noema, the expectations which are carried may be frustrated (as when the intended object does not exist); those expectations may be indeterminate; and, because the noema gives only a "one-sided" view of the intended object, there will be other possible descriptions corresponding to other possible noemata, all of which are "true of" the intended object, but none of which need be a description of the noema of this particular act.

But although Husserl's "noema" shares these characteristics of Anscombe's "intentional object", the one cannot be identified with the other. For the relation between Anscombe's "intentional" and "material" objects[24] cannot be the same as the relation between the noema and intended object. This becomes clear in the case of perception — the paradigm case of a psychological act which achieves objective reference.

Perception in the sense which Brentano called "outer perception" and which, in Anscombe's case, we described as "transparent" perception, is described by Husserl as a "transcendently directed"

---

[22] *Ibid.*

[23] *Supra*, Chapter IV.

[24] Anscombe, of course, is unable to state what this relation *is*. But her characterisation of "intentional" and "material" objects, respectively, enables us to say what this relation can*not* be.

act. Because the object of perception in this sense is a transcendent object, that object *can only* be given "one-sidedly" in a particular act. So the sense in which the noema is "not the same thing" as the intended object, is the sense in which the mode in which something is intended is different from the thing itself. The difference here is not that between a "transcendently directed" act and an "immanently directed" act, where the latter is an act in which the object is wholly given. The three-levelled framework against which the notion of noema is set, is one which allows us to say that the noema is not the same thing as the intended object, without thereby relegating to the noema the status of an object which is immanently contained within an act. (Analogously, in Frege's case, we can distinguish sense from reference without thereby relegating sense to the realm of ideas). Anscombe's distinction of "intentional" and "material" objects at times seems closer to Husserl's distinction between immanently and transcendently directed acts rather than to his account of the relation between noema and intended (i.e., transcendent) object: When she identifies the "merely intentional" use of "perceives" with the sense-impression theorists' use, then perceiving here is to be regarded as an immanently directed act (in Husserl's terminology). Although it is true to say that the sense-impression theorists' account of perceiving corresponds to Husserl's "immanently directed" act, the latter could not on Husserl's account be described as a case of a "merely intentional" use of "perceives". For an immanently directed act is one in which an object is given non-perspectivally — it is, like Brentano's presentations, to be understood in terms of the dichotomy of act and object. It is precisely that dichotomy which is denied by Husserl in characterising intentionality by appeal to the noema.

In Anscombe's case the identification of perceiving in its merely intentional sense with an immanently directed act yields consequences which are incompatible with her thesis concerning objective reference in the case of transparent perception (where "perceives" is used materially). For here Anscombe wants to say there is an intentional object but that this is not something other than, or in addition to, the real existing thing. To retain what she takes to be correct about sense-impression theories, Anscombe treats an "intentional object" as an "immanent object" (in

152

Husserl's sense). To retain what she takes to be correct about realist theories (the primacy of the material use of "perceives"), she attempts to say that the intentional object is nothing other than the real, existing thing. Neither of these theses allows for the possibility of treating the "intentional object" as *a means to* achieving objective reference in cases where "perceives" is used materially. This is because Anscombe's account is couched in terms of a dichotomy of

act — object,

rather than in terms of a trichotomy which allows an "intentional object" to be treated as *the means by which* we intend something objective. Appeal to Husserl's distinction between transcendently-directed and immanently-directed acts shows us why Anscombe's account of intentionality is fundamentally incompatible with her thesis that psychological acts, such as perceiving, can succeed in achieving objective reference; appeal to Husserl's notion of the noema shows us that this incompatibility can only be resolved by replacing the dichotomy of act and object by a trichotomy in which the intentional (i.e., the noema) is a means to achieving objective reference.

Husserl's account of the perspectival nature of perception might also be invoked to defend Frege against the charge of scepticism in relation to his thesis that, because sense gives us only a one-sided view of the reference, we can never attain full knowledge of that reference.[25] If the reference (of a name), which is known by means of the sense, is transcendent in the way that for Husserl the intended object of perceiving is, then it is something which can *only* be given perspectivally. To require that it be completely — i.e. non-perspectivally — given is to require that "knowing the reference" be an immanently-directed act.[26] It is interesting to note here that Russell's account of "knowing the reference" fulfils this requirement. For Russell, the reference of a name is something

[25] *Supra*, p. 39.

[26] Ameriks (1977) points out: "Husserl recognizes that the epistemic transcendence things have in the sense of not being completely given is not in itself a proof of a real transcendence in the sense of a separate existence. At this point . . . he is simply trying to . . . ward off an ideal knowledge which would require the perception of transcendent things to have precisely what is impossible, namely the character of immanent perception" (p. 501).

that is known non-perspectivally – without mediation. This is required if we are to say in the case of names that the reference is known incorrigibly. But on this account the reference which is known must be something immanent to the act of knowing so that, in this context, Russell's theory of names is unmistakably a psychologistic theory.

We can now return to Husserl's theory of the intentionality of perception, and summarise it as follows: The noema or meaning of a perceptual act is the mode in which the object is intended in that particular act. The object which is perceived is a *correlate* of an intentional act. The relation between an act and its intended object is an intentional relation – one that is mediated by a noema or sense.

This account of Husserl's theory of the intentionality of perception shows us how sense or meaning can be understood as "mind-related". For here the notion of sense plays a crucial role in our understanding of the intentionality of acts of consciousness. We are now in a position to see how this theory might account for the "mind-relatedness" of linguistic meaning – i.e., the sense of linguistic expressions. Referring to something by means of a linguistic expression is one of many possible intentional acts. The linguistic act in *"A refers to B"* (by means of some linguistic expression) is, like the perceptual act in *"A perceives B"*, an instance of *A*'s intending some object, *B*. On Husserl's account, linguistic reference – the relation between a sign and its referent – is to be understood in terms of an act which has the structure:

act – meaning (noema) – object.

What we have, here, is a theory about acts. Meaning, construed as noema, is a notion developed in relation to acts. For Frege, meaning or *Sinn* is, more specifically, linguistic meaning – a notion which applies to linguistic expressions. If Husserl's noematic approach to the meaning of acts is to serve as the required supplement to Frege's theory of sense, then we must first be able to demonstrate the way in which a theory of acts is capable of yielding a theory of linguistic meaning. Second, we must be able to show that the notion of meaning that is so yielded is, in fact, equivalent to that of Frege's – that it is anti-psychologistic in the way insisted on by Frege. Finally, we must go beyond this and show how an appeal to the intentionality of acts can serve to rehabilitate the notion of Fregean *Sinn* in the face of the kind of criticisms levelled by Putnam.[27]

The theory of meaning which is articulated in Husserl's earlier work – his *Logical Investigations*[28] – provides a programme for implementing the first of these requirements, and articulates a notion of meaning which is quite explicitly designed to satisfy the second (*viz.* to establish "meaning" as an anti-psychologistic notion in precisely Frege's sense). For these reasons, Husserl's early account of linguistic meaning in *Logical Investigations* merits some attention. But this account, although free of one kind of psychologism, is arguably still vulnerable to another kind – *viz.*, psychologism of the kind objected to by Putnam. Husserl, in *Logical Investigations*, is said to assume a "one-sidedly noetic" approach[29] – an approach which requires that investigations into meaning be understood ultimately as investigations into psychological acts. Subsequent to this work, Husserl introduced his distinction of *noesis* and *noema*, and thereby opened up the possibility of a new kind of investigation into the meaning which is associated with acts, *viz.*, an investigation into the noematic correlates of those acts. This "noematic" approach to meaning was fully developed in Husserl's *Ideas* of 1913. In the light of this subsequent development, Husserl's early approach can be seen as falling short of a conclusive defence against psychologism. It is for this reason that Husserl's noematic approach to meaning which we have described in §2 above must be the ultimate court of appeal in this defence. The significance of the noematic approach of *Ideas* for such a defence becomes clear when it is contrasted with the earlier noetic approach of *Logical Investigations* which serves as our point of departure is discussing the relation of acts to linguistic meaning.

§3. *Intentional acts and linguistic meaning: a noetic approach*

Husserl introduces his theory of linguistic ("expressive") meaning in *Logical Investigations* by distinguishing between the sign as

[27] These are the criticisms elaborated in Chapter V, above.

[28] Husserl (1900–1901). The version of this work which is relied on in this chapter is J.N. Findlay's translation of the second edition which was published in 1913, the same year as the publication of *Ideas I*.

[29] De Boer (1978); Bernet (1979). The "noema" was explicitly introduced for the first time in 1904. See De Boer (1978), p. 317n.

physical phenomenon and the sign as meaningful expression. What makes the mere physical sign a meaningful expression is the interpolation of an act:

> If we seek a foothold in pure description, the concrete phenomenon of the sense-informed expression breaks up, on the one hand, into the *physical phenomenon* forming the physical side of the expression, and, on the other hand, into *acts* which give it *meaning* and possibly also *intuitive fulness,* in which its relation to an expressed object is constituted.[30]

A phenomenal sign – a concatenation of letters or a sequence of sounds – becomes an "expression" – a meaning-endowed sign – with the performance of an act of intending something objective – what Husserl calls an act of meaning-intending. A meaningful sign – an expression – is therefore but the public aspect of a particular act of intending something. It is in virtue of this act that the expression means something, and insofar as it means something, it relates to something objective. This "something objective" is the objective correlate[31] of the expression. When this "objective something" is actually given in accompanying acts of intuitive fulfilment, then the relation between the expression and its object is said to be realised. Alternatively, the expression may "lack any basic intuition that will give it its object",[32] in which case the expression still functions significantly – it is still a meaning-endowed sign – but its relation to an object is unrealised.

> A *name*, e.g., names its object whatever the circumstances, in so far as it *means* that object. But if the object is not intuitively before one, and so not before one as a named or meant object, mere meaning is all there is to it.[33]

[30] Husserl (1900–1901), p. 280 of Findlay's translation of the second German edition (1913).

[31] In a note (*ibid.*, p. 281n.), Husserl remarks that he "often make(s) use of the vaguer expression 'objective correlate', (*Gegenständlichkeit*) since we are never limited to objects in the narrower sense, but have also to do with states of affairs, properties . . .".

[32] *Ibid.*, p. 280.

[33] *Ibid.*

So for example, in meaningfully uttering the expression 'the present king of France", I perform an act of meaning-intending. The objective correlate of the expression is the object I intend in uttering that expression meaningfully. In this particular case, where there is no such object, my meaning intention is said to remain empty or unfulfilled: the relation between the expression and its objective correlate is unrealised. If we move from the level of talk about expressions and their correlates to the level of talk about acts, then we can express this same point by saying that my act of meaning-intending is not accompanied by acts of meaning fulfilment. The meaning intention of my act is not fulfilled in accompanying intuitions. The particular acts of meaning fulfilment are, for Husserl, perception and imagination. These acts may provide complete fulfilment (as in cases where what is intended is something self-evident) or they may provide only partial fulfilment. Although acts of meaning fulfilment may accompany acts of meaning intending, they are not constituents of meaning. For, as we have seen in the case of "the present king of France", an act of meaning-intending is performed − a meaning intention or intending sense has been expressed − but there are no accompanying acts of meaning fulfilment. The meaning intention remains empty.

In the case of the expression "the present king of France", the absence of meaning fulfilment is a function of empirical circumstances − my utterance of this expression at this particular time in history. In the case of expressions like "round square" although, once again, there is an act of meaning intending, this intention is *a priori* incapable of fulfilment. However, in the case of expressions like "the president of the U.S.A. in 1979" where there is something answering to the name or description, then we can say that the relation between the expression and its objective correlate is realised or that the intention expressed is fulfilled, if that object is given in the manner intended in accompanying acts of intuition: "If the originally empty meaning intention is now fulfilled, the relation to an object is realised, the naming becomes an actual conscious relation between the name and the object named".[34]

We might remark at the outset that in this analysis of an "act-based" theory of linguistic meaning, Husserl's examples of

[34] *Ibid.*, p. 281.

meaningful expressions are referring expressions – nouns and noun-phrases. Husserl calls them "names". But clearly it is the Fregean rather than the Russellian sense of "name" that Husserl exploits. For a name is still meaningful regardless of whether or not there exists any object named by it. Moreover, when the object does exist (is "intuitively before one . . ."), it is by virtue of the *meaning* of the expression that the relation between the name and its objective correlate is realised.

In summary we can say that, for Husserl, linguistic reference – the relation between a sign and its referent – is an intentional relation consisting of

(expressive) sign – meaning – objective correlate.

This is so because linguistic reference is to be understood in terms of an underlying intentional act. An intentional act, as we have seen, has the following structure:

act – meaning – object.

According to the theory proposed in *Logical Investigations*, the specific act which "animates" a sign – the act of meaning-intending – has the following structure:

acts of meaning-intending – meaning intention – object.
(meaning content)

The notion of meaning which occurs here has the objective status of Frege's "thought", and to this extent, Husserl's theory of meaning escapes the psychologistic consequences to which Frege drew objection. Frege, we may recall, had accused Husserl of transforming everything into the subjective by blurring the boundary between the subjective and objective. He insisted that a genuinely non-psychologistic theory of logical laws and concepts must show that what is grasped in understanding is objective – i.e. a "thought" – in *contrast* to what is subjective.[35]

Frege's own way of characterizing the objectivity of the thought is one that appeals to an ontological distinction between ideas (which are subjective) and thoughts (which are objective). For Frege, ideas belong to the inner realm. They cannot be

---

[35] Frege (1894), pp. 324–5.

perceived by the senses. Ideas "are had" — that is, they cannot exist independently on one who "has" the idea. Ideas can be the content of only one consciousness in a way which makes it impossible to speak of someone else's having "the same" idea as mine. They are non-repeatable, non-shareable and private. This entails, for Frege, the impossibility of their being amenable to judgements of truth and falsity.

By contrast, a thought is that to which we can ascribe truth and falsity.[36] Thoughts are true or false independently of subjective beliefs. Thoughts, such as the Pythagorean theorem, are publicly recognizable and publicly shareable. They are not the private contents of individual minds. Thoughts are, however, not perceivable through the senses and are not, therefore, members of the "outer realm" of material perceptible objects. They are abstract entities. Frege says that thoughts belong to a "third realm" in that they display features of both the inner and outer realms.

Frege's ontological characterisation of the thought tells us what it means to say that the thought is objective — it tells us the characteristics which mark off the thought from the private and subjective. In this respect it states a "criterion of adequacy" for a non-psychologistic theory about the relation between meaning and the mind: Meaning must have the objectivity of the thought.

This criterion is satisfied in the case of Husserl's theory of linguistic meaning. The meaning content of an act is not to be identified with the act itself: the meaning of an expression, for example, "quadratic remainder", is not an unrepeatable sound-pattern, but neither is to be identified with a particular meaning-conferring experience. The meaning of "quadratic remainder" is something that remains the same no matter how many times I utter it, and no matter how many different people utter it (meaningfully). The meaning of an expression is that which remains the same throughout a plurality of individual intending acts.

Husserl gives us examples of cases of asserting and judging. If I assert that the three perpendiculars of a triangle intersect at a point, I do so on the basis of a judgement that this is so. But the meaning of *what* I assert is not to be explained by reference to my particular, subjective act of judging. What I assert is something

[36] Frege (1918), pp. 4–5.

which remains the same no matter who may judge of it, and no matter on what occasion:

> One therefore repeats what is in essence 'the same' assertion, and one repeats it because it is the one uniquely adequate way of expressing the same thing, i.e., its meaning ... What we assert in the judgement involves nothing subjective. My act of judging is a transient experience: it arises and passes away. But what my assertion asserts, the content *that the three perpendiculars of a triangle intersect at a point*, neither arises nor passes away. It is an identity in the strict sense, one and the same geometrical truth.[37]

If the meaning of an expression is to be identified with the particular individual act which expresses it, then our account of meaning is a psychologistic one. For meaning, in this case, would be a temporal event which comes to be and which ceases to be with the temporal event of the utterance which expresses it; there would be a plurality of meanings corresponding to the plurality of concrete individual acts. The meaning-content is not a "real" (*reell*), concrete, temporal event, in the way in which acts themselves are; nor is it "real" (*real*) in the sense in which transcendent objects are. Because meanings are not real in either of these senses, Husserl says that they are "ideal".[38] Because the same self-identical content is expressible in a plurality of individual acts, Husserl speaks of meaning as a "unity". Hence the meaning of an expression — the self-identical meaning-content which can be brought to expression in a plurality of real individual acts — is said to be an "ideal unity".

By characterising the distinction of acts and their contents as a distinction of real events as opposed to ideal unities, Husserl can

---

[37] Husserl (1900–1901), p. 285 of Findlay's translation of the second German edition (1913). *Cf.* Frege (1918a), p. 42n.: "We are probably best in accord with ordinary usage if we take a judgement to be an act of judging as a leap is an act of leaping... Judging, we may say, is acknowledging the truth of something; what is acknowledged to be true can only be thought ... If a judgement is an act, it happens at a certain time and thereafter belongs to the past".

[38] McIntyre & Smith (1975), p. 119.

avoid psychologism of the kind opposed by Frege. The meaning of an expression – the intending sense – is, like Frege's "thought", shareable, atemporal and, in the case of propositional meaning, capable of being judged true or false. Husserl's "meaning", in other words, is successfully marked off from the private, temporal, subjective act.

However, Husserl's way of distinguishing the objective (the meaning-content of an expression) from the subjective (the individual act) is very different from Frege's way of distinguishing the thought from the subjective idea or image. Frege's distinction is one which invokes the notion of ontological realms; Husserl's distinction is drawn phenomenologically – that is, by appeal to a phenomenological description of the intentionality of acts.

Moreover, for Husserl, it was only by means of phenomenological analysis that the psychologistic blurring of the logical and the psychological could be avoided: Husserl sees the task of philosophy as that of clarifying the concepts and laws of pure logic. Pure logic is the science of ideal meanings or "essences". Phenomenological investigation is said to be a necessary preliminary to the task of clarification, for

> Phenomenology . . . lays bare the 'sources' from which the basic concepts and ideal laws of pure logic 'flow', and back to which they must once more be traced, so as to give them all the 'clearness and distinctness' needed for an understanding and for an epistemological critique, of pure logic.[39]

Husserl is careful to dissociate phenomenological analysis from descriptive psychology[40] or from any of the empirical sciences. Phenomenology, by investigating essences or the *a priori* structures of thought and knowledge experiences is, in fact, a way of combating psychologism which results from the confusion of the logical with the psychological:

[39] Husserl (1900–1901), pp. 249–50 of Findlay's translation of second German edition (1913). It is only at the stage of this second edition that Husserl begins to articulate a clear statement of a *phenomenological* programme in place of the "descriptive psychology" of the first edition (1900–1901) of the *Logical Investigations*.

[40] There are disputes concerning whether or not *in fact* Husserl was successful in doing this. See De Boer (1978), pp. 286–7.

Psychologism can only be radically overcome by a pure phenomenology, a science infinitely removed from psychology as the empirical science of the mental attributes and states of animal realities. In . . . the sphere of pure logic, such a phenomenology alone offers us all the necessary conditions for a finally satisfactory establishment of the totality of basic distinctions and insights. It alone frees us from the strong temptation . . . to turn the logically objective into the psychological.[41]

If the mind-relatedness of meaning is explained by appeal to a phenomenological theory about acts then it can escape the charge of psychologism of the kind levelled by Frege. But is it nonetheless a psychologistic notion in Putnam's sense? For Putnam, a psychologistic theory of meaning is one which states that meaning is determined by psychological state. The theories under criticism, we will recall,[42] include those which idealize meanings by characterizing them as abstract entities: The grasping of these entities is still a psychological act. Any theory which holds that investigations into meaning are ultimately investigations into psychological acts is, therefore, vulnerable to this criticism.

Husserl's disclaimer notwithstanding, there would seem to be a reasonable case for urging this objection against his theory of meaning in *Logical Investigations*. For here, meaning is ultimately a property of acts. Specifically, what this means is that meaning is inwardly determined by the act's "intentional essence".[43] The intentional essence of an act comprises two elements, quality and matter. These components can be discerned in the following set of utterances: (1) "There are intelligent beings on Mars"; (2) "Are there intelligent beings on Mars?"; (3) "If only there were intelligent beings on Mars!" The difference between these utterances is a difference in the quality of the respective acts (i.e., asserting, questioning, wishing, etc.). The 'content' which remains the same is the matter of the act.[44]

[41] Husserl (1900–1901), p. 253 of Findlay's translation of the second German edition (1913).

[42] *Supra*, pp. 134–135.

[43] Husserl (1900–1901). See Investigation V, especially pp. 586ff. of Findlay's translation of the second German edition (1913).

[44] Because no act can lack either quality or matter, these "inner constituents" are said to be "essential" − to comprise the act's (intentional) *essence*.

The sameness of content, here, must be explained in terms of something intrinsic to the act rather than in terms of the object, for, "The object is an intentional object: This means there is an act having a determinate intention, and determinate in a way which makes it an intention to this object".[45] For Husserl, it is the matter which determines the act's direction to the particular object it has. But, further to this, Husserl argues that the matter of the act is what determines meaning: Acts may differ whilst both quality and objective reference remain the same. The same object is intended by the expressions, "equilateral triangle" and "equiangular triangle" when these occur separately in acts which are qualitatively the same, e.g. two judgements. The difference must be a difference in the *matter* of the respective acts. It is therefore the difference in the *matter* of the two acts which determines the difference in the *meaning* of the two expressions:

> The matter, therefore, must be *that element in an act which first gives it reference to an object, and reference so wholly definite that it not merely fixes the object meant in a general way, but also the precise way in which it is meant.* The matter . . . is that peculiar side of an act's phenomenological content that not only determines *that* it grasps the object, but also *as what* it grasps it, . . .[46]

As De Boer points out: "the matter indicates that the act is inwardly determined by the property to intend a particular object".[47]

In short, the approach to meaning which Husserl develops in the *Logical Investigations* is one in which meaning, although not a real component of acts, is nonetheless a property of acts in the sense that it is ultimately determined (inwardly) by the act's intentional essence. It follows from this that investigations into meaning are ultimately investigations into psychological acts. This way of approaching the intentionality of "meaning" is therefore inadequate to meet Putman's objections.

[45] *Ibid.*, p. 587.
[46] *Ibid.*, p. 589.
[47] De Boer (1978), p. 143.

If we are to rehabilitate Frege's notion of sense *vis-à-vis* these objections, it is not necessary that we abandon a phenomenological theory of the intentionality of meaning. Rather, we must turn from a one-sidedly *noetic* approach to meaning (an "act-based" approach) to a *noematic* one (an approach involving the *correlates* of those acts). We have already seen in §2 above what Husserl's theory of the noema consists in. Our task now is to show the significance of such a theory for a genuinely non-psychologistic theory of Fregean sense.

§4. *The sense and reference of names: a noematic approach*

The Fregean semantic theory with its trichotomy of

1. sign – sense – reference

is to be explained by appeal to acts which have the tripartite structure of

2. act – meaning – object.

The notion of "meaning" which occurs in this structure can admit of the noetic approach of *Logical Investigations* which we discussed in §3 above:

2'. act of meaning-intending – *meaning content* – object.

Alternatively, it can admit of a noematic approach of the kind elaborated in §2 above, in relation to *Ideas*:

2''. act – *noema* – object.

The turn from the noetic approach (2') to the noematic approach (2'') requires a transition from the level of discourse about acts to the level of discourse about what is "given in" those acts – to what Husserl in *Ideas* calls the noematic correlates of acts. This transition is recognized in *Logical Investigations*.[48] However,

---

[48] De Boer (1978) points out that Husserl *implicitly* recognizes the possibility of a noematic approach in *Logical Investigations,* especially in relation to fulfilling acts – i.e. acts, like perception, for which there are correlates. In connection with the transition from a noetic to a noematic approach it must be emphasized that the possibility of a noematic approach requires the methodological apparatus of the phenomenological *epoché* discussed in §2 above.

without the apparatus of the noesis-noema distinction, its consequences for "correlative analysis" cannot be exploited.

We have seen, in this earlier work, how to every act of meaning-intending there corresponds a meaning intention through which some object[49] is intended. It is in virtue of such an act that an expression can be said to have a meaning – the *intending sense* of the expression – through which it relates to something objective – the *objective correlate* of the expression. For Husserl the meaning of an expression, which is an ideal unity, is not to be identified with the act itself which is a concrete, temporal, real (*reell*) event. Without departing from the phenomenological standpoint, we can distinguish between the particular act and the "content" of that act. But when we move to the level of discourse about the "contents" of acts – what is "given in" these acts – we have a further distinction to make. If we look at what is given in these acts, we discern not only the meaning content but also the objective correlate of the act:

> Every expression not merely says something, but says it *of* something: it not only has a meaning, but refers to certain *objects*. This relation sometimes holds in the plural for one and the same expression, but the object never coincides with the meaning. Both, of course, only pertain to an expression in virtue of the mental acts which give it sense. And, if we distinguish between 'content' and object in respect of such 'presentations', one's distinction means the same as the distinction between what is *meant* or said, on the one hand, and what is spoken *of*, on the other.[50]

It is this turn to what is "given in" acts which yields for Husserl a distinction between the meaning (*Bedeutung*) of an expression and the object referred to (*Gegenstand*) which parallels Frege's distinction between the sense (*Sinn*) and reference (*Bedeutung*) of an expression.[51] Husserl, like Frege, remarks on the a-symmetry of

[49] Husserl's term is "Gegenstand" – the named or referred. See Mohanty (1964), p. 17.

[50] Husserl (1900–1901), p. 287 of Findlay's translation of the second German edition (1913).

[51] Note the terminological difference: Husserl's *Bedeutung* is equivalent to Frege's *Sinn*; Frege's *Bedeutung* is equivalent to Husserl's *Gegenstand*.

sense and reference – the fact that expressions with different senses can refer to the same object. Like Frege, Husserl points out that the sense of an expression cannot be identified with the object referred to, because an expression may have a sense (be meaningful) even though there *exist* no object to which that expression refers. We can speak meaningfully about objects which do not exist, such as "Pegasus" or "round squares". Finally, for Husserl, as for Frege, meaning is a determinant of the reference of an expression:

> An expression only refers to an objective correlate *because* it means something; it can be rightly said to signify or name the object *through* its meaning. An act of meaning is the determinate manner in which we refer to our object of the moment, though this mode of significant reference and the meaning itself can change, while the objective reference remains fixed.[52]

Here we see that Husserl's theory about *acts* of referring to (i.e., intending) some object yields, as its logical consequence, a particular theory of *semantic* reference, that is, a theory of the relation between a name (a *linguistic* item) and the object referred to. The particular theory of semantic reference here is the Fregean one, which entails that to every name there is correlated a sense or meaning: Where a name N, refers to something objective, O, the relation, "N refers to O" is a relation that is mediated by sense or meaning.

However, on Husserl's theory, "meaning" or "sense" is an intentional notion – a notion tied to his theory of the intentionality of acts. At this level, referring is an instance of an intentional *act* and must be seen as a relation between the subject of an act – i.e., some person – and the object intended in that act. We can say that, at this level, we have a theory of "personal" reference which, in Husserl's case, is the theory that the relation between a person (the one who

[52] *Ibid.*, p. 289.

uses the name) and an object referred to is an intentional relation.[53]

In short, we can say that a Fregean theory of semantic reference is, in Husserl's case, sustained by a theory of "personal" reference, specifically that theory which states that A's referring to O by means of some expression is an instance of A's intending O. A noematic reading of this underlying act requires that we construe such an act in terms of the structure

act — noema — object.

In the terminology of *Ideas*, A's referring to some object, O, is a transcendently-directed act.[54] This, as we have seen, is not equivalent to the claim that the object must exist. Rather, the object *which* is referred to can only be given "perspectivally". (If the object were wholly given, then the act would be immanently directed). The object *as* referred to in a particular act is the meaning, i.e., noema, of that act. With the performance of the phenomenological *epoché*, what we are left with is not merely an act but the "meant (or referred to) as such", the intentional object which is correlated with the act, that is, the noema.

The terminology of "object which is referred to" and "object as referred to", although borrowed from *Logical Investigations*[55] is, in fact, more appropriate to the methodological framework of *Ideas*. For it signifies a turn away from the acts themselves to the

[53] Husserl's theory of personal reference must, however, be distanced from those theories of personal reference offered by e.g., Grice and Searle, and by Donnellan (1966). Although these theories appeal to the notion of "speaker's intentions" or "beliefs/information associated with name", they are set within a two-levelled semantical framework — one which either (a) prevents us from saying that linguistic sense or meaning is the "expressed meaning intention of an act" (Grice, Donnellan) or (b) commits us to identifying the sense of a name with the descriptions into which a name can be analyzed (in the manner of Russell's Theory of Descriptions). The discussions of Altham (1973) and Evans (1973) show that these theories are genuine instances of the "description theory" of names — a theory set against the two-levelled semantical framework. See Appendix B.

[54] *Supra*, p. 148.

[55] Husserl (1900—1901), p. 578 of Findlay's translation of the second German edition (1913).

"objects", i.e. correlates, of those acts.[56] The relation of the "object as referred to" to the "object which is referred to" is the relation of the noema to the objective reference. A genuine correlative analysis is now possible. For investigations into the relation between the noema and the objective reference are investigations into the noematic structures of acts — i.e., investigations into the correlates of acts.

The fact that the object which is referred to can remain identical while the object as referred to changes is explained by the fact that "we can be directed toward one and the same object as its properties are changing. The object is then the identity pole of a number of perceptions whose noema is changing; it is the bearer of the properties".[57]

It is this aspect of the relation of noema to object which, at the semantic level, explains the a-symmetry of sense and reference. At the same time, it explains why we can say that sense is a determinant of reference without thereby making sense a property of an act (i.e., a property — that of being directed toward a particular object — which is "inwardly determined" by the act-matter).

A noematic approach to meaning permits a correlative analysis even in the case of signifying acts — those acts of "mere meaning". In the terminology of *Logical Investigations*, these are the acts whose meaning intention remains "empty". As De Boer points out: "In *Logical Investigations* there was a correlation between act and object only in the case of intuitive acts (acts of meaning fulfilment), while acts of mere meaning really had no correlates. There was no objective significative meaning corresponding to

[56] Husserl's "ideal unities" (§3, above) are not correlates of acts. Their relation to individual acts is that of "*eidos* to fact" De Boer (1978), pp. 252ff. It is a relation comparable to that between redness and individual instances of redness. The notion of "ideal unities" belongs to noetic investigations, specifically, investigations into the *idea* of the (judging) act rather than into the objective *correlates* of those acts. See also Bernet (1979).

[57] This is not to claim that the object is "reducible" to a set of properties. For, given our notion of a transcendently-directed act, the object cannot be the same thing as the noema. Nor, at the other extreme, can we claim that the object somehow stands "behind" the noemata: "The noemata refer to the identity pole as the most inward moment of each separate noema, which at the same time binds them together as the properties of this one object" De Boer (1978), p. 449.

them. But in *Ideas I,* Husserl also accepts a correlate in the case of acts of mere meaning. This is the objective meaning . . .".[58]

A semantic theory, like that of Frege and Husserl, which states that to every name there corresponds a sense can, therefore, be understood by appeal to the notion of an intentional act of referring to some object. If the "meaning" of this underlying act is interpreted noematically — i.e. as a correlate of the act, rather than a property which is inwardly determined by the essence of the act — then we can assert that the notion of sense which enters into our semantic theory is not psychologistic in the way alleged by Putnam.

Putnam claims that sense is a psychologistic notion because, as traditionally understood, it is a notion belonging to psychology: Investigations into meaning or sense are ultimately investigations into a psychological state. Putnam distinguishes two senses of "psychological state"[59] — a wide sense and a narrow sense. A psychological state in the wide sense is one which is studied or described by psychology. Investigations into meaning-as-noema cannot be considered as investigations into psychological states in *this* sense, however, for it is not the psychological *act* that is the subject-matter of such inquiries but, rather, the *objects,* i.e. *correlates,* of those acts. Investigations into meaning are not psychological investigations — they are *correlative* analyses.

Nor can it be claimed that meaning-as-noema can be associated with psychological states in Putnam's narrow sense. For a psychological state in this sense is one in which the object of an act is regarded as immanent to the act.[60] As Putnam points out, many cases of what we ordinarily mean by "psychological state" will have to be radically reconstructed if they are to be treated as psychological states in the narrow sense. Putnam gives the example of jealousy: ". . . In its ordinary use, *x is jealous of y* entails *y* exists, and *x is jealous of y's regard for z* entails that both *y* and *z* exist (as well as *x,* of course) . . .".[61] Taken this way, jealousy can

---

[58] De Boer (1978), p. 443; See also pp. 171, 285, 296.

[59] Putnam (1975).

[60] One might argue that even the notion of meaning in *Logical Investigations* was not psychologistic in Putnam's "narrow sense" which requires meaning to be a real (*reell*) component of the temporal, subjective act.

[61] Putnam (1975), p. 220.

be called a psychological state in the "wide sense". But, if we are to treat jealousy as a psychological state in the narrow sense, then we must "reconstrue *jealousy* so that I can be jealous of my own hallucinations or figments of my imagination, etc.".[62]

If object-directed psychological acts were to be described as psychological states in Putnam's narrow sense, then they would have to be construed as "immanently directed" acts, in Husserl's terminology, and therefore be understood in terms of a dichotomy of act and object. Because, for Husserl, acts such as x's being jealous of y are intentional acts which are to be analysed in terms of the trichotomy of act, noema (meaning) and object, they cannot be psychological states in Putnam's narrow sense.

At the level of semantic reference, both Husserl and Frege accept the thesis that there can be names which have a sense but which do not refer to anything. This means that, at the level of personal reference, we must admit the possibility of "unsuccessful" reference — that is to say, the possibility of using a name meaningfully even though there exists nothing to which that name refers (in the semantic sense), e.g., "Pegasus".[63] Frege's own concerns were confined to the level of semantic reference, so that, although

---

[62] *Ibid.* As Putnam sees it, this kind of reconstruction is necessitated by the assumption of methodological solipsism, *viz.*, the assumption that "no psychological state . . . presupposes the existence of any individual other than the subject to whom that state is ascribed" (*ibid.*). Stated this way, the assumption appears to be compatible with the phenomenological principle which demands freedom from presuppositions. But, if we *do* impute this assumption to Husserl, then we cannot say that it is a principle necessitating re-construction of object-directed psychological acts as psychological states in Putnam's *narrow* sense. Putnam, however, clearly takes the principle of methodological solipsism as one deriving from the Cartesian method of doubt: ". . . in fact the assumption was that no psychological state presupposes the existence of the subject's *body* even", and adds: "This assumption was pretty explicit in Descartes, but it is implicit in just about the whole of traditional philosophical psychology (*ibid.*). If the principle of methodological solipsism is one which itself presupposes Cartesian doubt, then it cannot be the same principle as that of a presuppositionless approach or of the *epoché*. For Descartes, the principle of methodological solipsism derives from the "denial of what is not known for certain; Husserl's suspension of belief is (a matter of) 'taking belief out of play'." Attig (1980), p. 22.

[63] The possibility of "unsuccessful reference" in this sense is, of course, not admitted in Russell's theory of names.

the possibility of "unsuccessful reference" (at the level of personal reference) is implied by his theory,[64] there is no account of what this might consist in. If, as we are urging, Frege's theory of semantic reference is to be supplemented by Husserl's theory of intentionality, then the latter must be one which allows us to distinguish between "successful" and "unsuccessful" reference. However, because at the level of personal reference, "refers" or "referring" is an intentional notion – one which does not presuppose or imply that the object referred to exists or does not exist – our distinction between successful and unsuccessful reference cannot be drawn by appeal to the existence or non-existence of what is referred to.[65]

We have already observed that the possibility of a correlative analysis does not depend upon the existence or otherwise of the object *which* is referred to in a particular act: A correlative analysis is possible even for signifying acts. In terms of such an analysis the contrast of "successful" and "unsuccessful" reference must be re-described as the justification or otherwise of the attribution of "real existence" to the object which is intended. Such justification in turn depends upon the harmony or otherwise of the noemata of a series of acts which all intend the same object. To each of these acts there corresponds a noema, but it is possible for the

[64] Furth (1964) reports that Frege suggest the following manner of speaking: " ... by the use of a name that denotes ('*bedeuten*') a certain object, a person *designates* ('*bezeichnen*') that object. Thus 'designates' would differ from 'denotes' in referring, not to a semantical property of an expression – the property, for example, that belongs to a complete name A if there exists an object x such that A denotes x – but rather to a certain use made by a person of an expression. 'The Parthenon' denotes the Parthenon; but by use of 'the Parthenon' I designate the Parthenon ..." (p.xlix). For Frege, a notion of personal reference must be recognised if the category of assertions is to be introduced to correspond to (acts of) judging. For judging is "my use of a sentence to assert that the denotation of which the thought it expresses is a sense *is* the True". *Ibid.* For Frege, assertions stand to judging in the way that names stand to designating: "The sense of a name of a truth-value I call a *thought*. I further say a name *expresses* its sense and *denotes* its denotation. I *designate* with the name that which it denotes". Frege (1893), p. 35.

[65] Husserl does in fact offer such an account in *Logical Investigations,* in terms of the fulfilment of the meaning intention of signifying acts. This account, however requires us to see the contrast between successful and unsuccessful reference solely in terms of the differentiation of *acts.*

noemata of the acts in this series to conflict with one another and to cancel each other out in which case "the object explodes and dissolves into contradictory appearances". Alternatively, the object may manifest itself in the noemata, as the identity pole of the "most inward moment" of each separate noema.[66]

For Frege reference, at the semantic level, requires the existence of an object. This may seem, *prima facie,* incompatible with a theory of personal reference in which reference (in the sense of intending some object) does not imply existence. This is not the case, however, for we can demonstrate that, if we are to accept Frege's notion of "names" as a class comprising *both* expressions which refer to some existing object *and* expressions which do not refer to anything, then, at the level of personal reference our theory of "reference" must be one which, like Husserl's, does not imply existence. To assist in showing this, I shall introduce the following conventions: In talking about reference at the semantic level – i.e., reference as a property of linguistic expressions – I shall use the convention "refers$_S$"; to indicate that reference is being talked about at the personal level, I shall use the convention "refers$_P$". Frege's theory of semantic reference states that:

$$N \text{ refers}_S \text{ to } o \longrightarrow (\exists x)\, x = o \text{ (where "}N\text{" is a name).}$$

Husserl's theory of personal reference states that:

(i) A refers to $o \longrightarrow\!\!\!/\!\!\!\!\rightarrow (\exists x)\, x = o$

and

(ii) A refers to $o \longrightarrow\!\!\!/\!\!\!\!\rightarrow - (\exists x)\, x = o$ (where "A" is some person).

On Frege's theory of semantic reference, the fact of the existence of some object associated with a name is necessary for that expression's being a sign which *refers$_S$*. But the fact of existence is not necessary to that expression's being a *name*. In this Frege differs from Russell, for whom the non-existence of the object means not only that there is no reference$_S$, but also that there is no name.

[66] De Boer (1978). See also *supra,* p. 148.

On Husserl's theory of personal reference, we can say that the class of names (a semantic category) is the class of expressions by means of which we refer$_p$. Because, at this level, referring$_p$ to something does not imply existence, the class of names will include both expressions which refer$_s$ to existing things as well as expressions which do not refer$_s$ to anything. Husserl's theory of referring$_p$ is, therefore, *compatible* with the theory of semantic reference which requires that reference implies existence, and it is a theory which *necessitates* that the category of names be one which admits names which do not refer$_s$ to anything.

Husserl's account, therefore, provides us with a way of answering the question: How is it that a name, such as "Pegasus", can be meaningful when it does not refer to anything? Russell's way of answering this was to deny that such expressions *are* names. Frege, as we have seen, tells us *that* names must have a sense but need not refer to anything. However, because Frege does not tell us how sense relates to the mind, his theory of sense is vulnerable to the charge of mentalism as we saw in the previous chapter. Husserl's theory of linguistic meaning and reference in terms of intentional acts provides us with the non-psychologistic theory of personal reference required to supplement Frege's theory in this respect.

RUSSELL'S ARGUMENTS FOR THE DISPENSIBILITY OF 'SENSE'

For Frege, failure of substitutivity *salva veritate* of co-referring expressions in certain contexts, is explained by appeal to the notion of "indirect reference". Indirect reference means, for Frege, reference to a sense: We may wish to speak about the sense of some expression, *p*. In this case, Frege says, the customary sense of "*p*" becomes the reference of our discourse.[1] In sentences containing quotation or reported speech, it is the (customary) *sense* of the subordinate expression that the words refer to. In such contexts, substitutivity, *salva veritate*, of co-referring expressions fails. It is only when words have their "customary reference" that the truth-value of the sentence can be preserved throughout substitutions of co-referring expressions which occur in that sentence.

The problem of sentences in which substitutivity fails is re-stated in Whitehead and Russell's *Principia Mathematica* as the problem of the "non-transparent occurrence" of a proposition. A proposition occurs "transparently" if that proposition is considered non-factually — that is to say, if "nothing is said about it, but by means of it something is said about something else."[2] A proposition which occurs transparently is a vehicle of truth or falsity. On the other hand, the occurrence of a proposition is said to be "non-transparent" if that proposition is considered factually — that is to say, if it is talked *about*: A proposition, *p*, occurs factually in "*A* believes *p*" or in "*p* is true". The proposition, in each of these

[1] Frege (1892), p. 59.
[2] Russell & Whitehead (1913), p. 407.

statements occurs non-transparently or factually. In such cases, we are talking about the symbol or the belief.

Quine, in *Word and Object*[3] coins the expression, "referential opacity" (or "non-transparency") to contrast with the notion of "referential transparency", where the latter notion, as Quine himself acknowledges, is derived straight from Whitehead and Russell. This contrast, for Quine, applies to sentential contexts. For Quine, the notion of "referentially transparent context" is tied to the notion of "purely referential position", that is to say, the position which is subject to substitutivity of identity. The position of "Tully" in the sentence, " 'Tully was a Roman' is trochaic" is not purely referential, for if we replace it by a co-designating term such as "Cicero", the truth-value of the containing sentence is disturbed. Because the occurrence of the singular term, here, is not purely referential, the construction in which it occurs is said to be a referentially opaque context. Referential transparency, therefore, is a feature of extensional constructions, for substitutivity is evidence of purely referential position on which transparency of context depends. Frege is the acknowledged inspiration behind Quine's basic notion of "purely referential position", here. But Quine adds a proviso to this acknowledgement, saying that "there is much in his (Frege's) associated theory that I do not adopt".[4]

What both Quine and Russell refuse to adopt is Frege's notion of sense. Although Russell and Quine are here talking about the same phenomenon as Frege — failure of substitutivity in the case of co-designating expressions — the re-casting of Frege's thesis of "indirect reference" as a thesis concerning "non-transparency" of occurrences or contexts has introduced minor but significant changes: (i) Whereas, for Frege, the thesis is stated in terms of "reference to a sense", in the Russell-Quine re-statement there is no mention of sense. (ii) Whereas Frege elaborates his thesis by appeal to the contrast of customary as opposed to indirect reference, Russell and Quine appeal instead to the contrast of transparent and non-transparent occurrences of propositions or contexts of sentences.

[3] Quine (1960), pp. 141ff.
[4] *Ibid.*, p. 142n.

The departure from Frege is more radical than this, however. The omission of Fregean "sense" from the Russell-Quine restatement of Frege's notion of "indirect reference" is part of a much stronger thesis, *viz.*, that sense is dispensable. The origins of this view are to be found in Russell's essay "On Denoting".[5] Here Russell mounts an explicit attack on what he takes to be Frege's notions of "sense" and "reference" and of the relation between them. Russell's arguments concerning the impossibility of referring to a sense are set against this background. In place of Frege's theory, Russell offers his own theory of denotation which, it is claimed, can solve certain problems surrounding the notion of reference without invoking the "mysterious" notion of sense. Russell translates Frege's "*Sinn*" as "meaning" and Frege's "*Bedeutung*" as "denotation". The significance of these terminological changes will be discussed later when we raise the question of whether it is, in fact, Frege's notions of "sense" and "reference" which are the targets for Russell's criticisms.

Russell interprets Frege's account of the relation between sense and reference as being the claim that this relation is a logical relation expressed by the following: "the meaning denotes the denotation". If it is not a logical relation then, as Russell sees it, it is "wholly mysterious". But the difficulty is that "we cannot succeed in *both* preserving the connexion of meaning and denotation *and* preventing them from being one and the same".[6] For Russell, this difficulty is demonstrated in attempts to talk about the meaning rather than the denotation of certain expressions. The failure of such attempts proves, for Russell, the impossibility of referring to the sense of an expression.

Russell singles out a particular class of denoting expressions to show this impossibility: These are definite descriptions of the kind, "the present king of France", "the first line of Gray's *Elegy*", "the centre of mass of the Solar system", etc. When phrases like these occur in a sentence, the sentence is about their denotation, when they have one. He says that if we wish to speak about the meaning of such phrases, then we do so by enclosing the phrase in inverted commas as follows:

[5] Russell (1905), pp. 479–93.
[6] *Ibid.*, p. 111.

The first line of Gray's *Elegy* states a proposition.

"The first line of Gray's *Elegy*" does not state a proposition.

If *C* represents the denoting phrase in the first of these examples, then we can say that when *C* occurs in a proposition, it is the denotation we are talking about. Hence, in the first of these sentences, we are talking about "The curfew tolls the knell of parting day". If we want to talk about the meaning of *C*, we put it in inverted commas, as in the second of the sentences given. But, by virtue of the logical relation between meaning and denotation — "meaning denotes a denotation" — if the meaning of *C* occurs in a proposition, then the proposition is about the denotation. Neither can we make "the meaning of '*C*'" the subject of our proposition. For "the meaning of '*C*'" is the same as '*C*' by itself and, if this occurs in a proposition then it is still the denotation that we are talking about, and not the meaning we want.

It is not just that none of our available locutions will allow us to denote the meaning we want — there can be no *possible* expression that will do the job. For the meaning of *C*, if it were genuinely referred to (i.e., denoted), would become a constituent of the proposition; meaning denotes a denotation; therefore the proposition would be about the denotation. For any expression that is claimed to successfully denote a meaning, we must give up the idea that there is a logical relation between the meaning of that expression and its denotation. In this case, Russell concludes, the relation remains "wholly mysterious".

Russell's attack on Frege and his own theory of denoting have been subjected to severe and protracted criticisms which need not concern us here. However, the objections raised by Searle[7] are of importance and interest to our present discussion. Searle criticises Russell's arguments (a) for the obscurities and inaccuracies — the latter being Russell's careless use of quotation marks; (b) for "an initial mis-statement of Frege's position",[8] combined with (c) a "persistent confusion between the notions of *occurring as part of a proposition* (being a constituent of a proposition) and *being*

---

[7] Searle (1958).

[8] *Ibid.*, p. 141. *Cf.*, Geach (1972), pp. 27–31.

referred to by a proposition".[9] He concludes that Russell performs a *reductio ad absurdum* on what is, in fact, a denial of Frege's account of the relation between sense and reference. It is the last two of these criticisms, (b) and (c), which concern us here.

Searle points out that Russell's arguments rest on the two "explicit assumptions", *viz.*, "(1) When we wish to refer to the sense of a referring expression we do so by enclosing the expression in inverted commas. (2) The sense of a referring expression refers to the referent".[10] The second of these is what Russell takes to be Frege's thesis concerning the relation of sense to reference. For Russell, the corollary of (2) is: (2a) "Whenever the sense of an expression *occurs in* a proposition, the proposition refers to the referent of that sense".[11]

Searle states that these two assumptions are not to be found in Frege's theory: First, enclosure by inverted commas is not sufficient to give us the sense of an expression. Rather, Frege says that we use the expression, "the sense of the expression '. . .'" to refer to the sense of an expression.[12] Second, it is not strictly true to say that Frege maintained that "meaning denotes the denotation". For Frege, it is the sign which refers, and it refers in virtue of its sense: A sign expresses a sense, and by means of this it refers to the referent. Hence Russell's corollary of this second assumption is also false: It is not the case that Frege believed that, when the sense of an expression *occurs in* a proposition, the proposition refers to the referent of that sense.

Russell's identification of "referent" with "constituent" of a proposition imports a notion of "occurring in a proposition" which is not present in Frege's own account of "sense" and "reference". Frege's account of the relation between sense and reference does not admit the possibility of a referent's "occurring in" (in Russell's sense) a proposition. It is the sign, and not the sense that refers. Every sign has a sense, and may or may not have a reference. It is by means of the sense that a sign refers. Thus if, on Frege's behalf, we can speak of *anything* "occurring in" a proposition, it will always be the sense and never the reference

---

[9] Searle (1958), p. 141.
[10] *Ibid.*, p. 137.
[11] *Ibid.*
[12] *Ibid.*, p. 138.

which occurs. Therefore, in the case of propositions containing an indirectly referring expression (one which refers to a sense) it is not the sense referred *to* that "occurs", but only the sense *by means of which* reference (in this case to a sense) is achieved.

These arguments demonstrate that Russell's notions of "meaning" and "denotation" are not the same as Frege's notions of "sense" and "reference". This is a consequence of (rather than a reason for) a misinterpretation of Frege's thesis concerning the relation of sign, sense and reference: it involves a failure to accept that, for Frege, sense is *a means by which* we refer.

Russell's misinterpretation of Frege's theory of sense and reference here, is a consequence of interpreting Frege's notions of "sense" and "reference" in terms of a two-levelled semantical framework — the framework of Russell's own theory of reference. Frege's notion of sense and his theory concerning the relation of sense to reference are tied, logically, to a three-levelled semantical framework. This means that (i) any attempt to locate Frege's theory of sense and reference within a two-levelled semantical framework will necessarily involve a distortion of that theory and of Frege's notion of sense. Within such a framework "sense" logically cannot be a means to determining reference, and "reference" logically cannot be that which is determined by sense; (ii) Russell's arguments for the dispensibility of Fregean sense within such a framework in fact beg the question. For his arguments assume a notion of reference as that which is not mediated by sense; and, yet, the arguments presented are designed to show that sense can be dispensed with — i.e., that it does not mediate reference.

APPENDIX B

THE CAUSAL THEORY OF NAMES

The causal theorists[1] accept what they take to be the essential insight of Russell's theory of names: a genuine name cannot fail in its mission to refer to a particular, existing individual; the capacity of guaranteeing reference is a logical feature of names; descriptions cannot guarantee reference. Causal theorists claim however to dispense with that aspect of Russell's own theory which they take to be unsatisfactory, *viz*., the Cartesian-derived epistemic necessity which, for Russell, formed the basis for his assertion that names guarantee reference. Russell's epistemological presuppositions are held to be double unsatisfactory. Not only do they lead to a psychologistic theory of reference – reference, in the case of names, being a function of acquaintance – but, in addition, they lead to the exclusion of ordinary proper names from the category of genuine names. Because the bearers of ordinary proper names are not objects of acquaintance (things whose existence is known for certain), ordinary names must be regarded as abbreviated descriptions. For causal theorists, then, the *necessity* of names' referring must not be confused with the epistemic notion of certainty.

Frege's thesis that every name necessarily has a sense is interpreted by the causal theorists to mean that every name is an abbreviated description (in the way in which, for Russell, ordinary proper names are). Frege's thesis that the reference of a name is determined by its sense is identified as a "description theory" of

---

[1] These are, primarily, Kripke (1972) and Putnam (1975); but they also include those like Altham (1973) and Evans (1973), who propose an "eclectic" version of the causal theory.

names. A description theory of names is one which holds that (i) every name is synonymous with a definite description (or set of such descriptions) true of at most one object, and (ii) the object which a name refers to is the object which (uniquely) instantiates the property or properties prescribed.[2]

The causal theory of names is proposed to replace or augment the so-called "description theory" of names.[3] It is argued that description theories do not do justice to the distinctive way in which names refer: Names necessarily succeed in referring to particulars. But a description can never succeed in doing this because any description or set of descriptions which purports to pick out a particular individual may, in fact, pick out the wrong individual or more than one individual, or perhaps, no individual at all. A genuine name, it is argued, cannot fail to refer in any of these ways. In the terminology of possible-worlds semantics, a name picks out the same individual in all possible worlds; for any given description, however, there are possible worlds in which that description will be satisfied by the wrong individual, or by more than one individual, or by no individual. Therefore, it is claimed that description theories are inadequate to explain reference in the case of a name.[4]

The causal theorists deny that "reference is determined by sense" (the latter being interpreted as a description theory of

---

[2] Included amongst the "description theorists" are Searle, Grice and Donnellan (1966), all of whom are seen as espousing a Fregean-derived theory of reference. More recently, (McIntyre (1978), (1982)), it has been suggested that Husserl might also be included among the description theorists. This is a result of (a) the perfectly legitimate move of identifying Husserl's theory of intentionality with Frege's theory of meaning, and (b) the assumption of a Russellian-derived interpretation of Frege's theory of sense and reference — an assumption which, in this thesis, I have attempted to show is unwarranted.

[3] It is not always clear whether causal theories are urged in order to "supplement the descriptive theory, to correct it, or both". Altham (1973), p. 210.

[4] Following this model, McIntyre (1978), (1982), and Smith (1982) point out that the "description-theory" interpretation of the Husserlian noema fails to do justice to the distinctive way in which the perceptual noema succeeds in achieving definiteness — in prescribing *which* object is intended in the act. They attempt a reconstruction of Husserl's theory on the model of a causal theory of names, (Smith and McIntyre (1982)), thereby retaining a fundamentally Russellian semantical framework. See Harney (1983).

names) and argue instead that reference, in the case of names, is causally determined. They argue as follows:

1. Names are what Kripke has called "rigid designators". That is to say, they have the capacity to pick out the same individual in all possible worlds in which that individual exists.

2. Names have this capacity because they are *indexicals*:

   (i) Indexicality is exemplified by demonstrative reference whereby the demonstrative is used to indicate, as opposed to describe, an object in the immediate sensory context of the utterer. Indicating is different from describing — it necessitates the *presence* of the object picked out by the indicating utterance, such that the relation between the utterance and the object indicated is a "direct" relation — one that is not mediated by descriptive information.

   (ii) Names (i.e., ordinary proper names) are said to be indexical because they are introduced by means of a demonstrative, as when we say, "This is Fred". Here, name-introduction is the conferral of a name *on what is indicated* by means of demonstrative reference (rather than on what is described).

3. The reference, which is fixed demonstratively in the introduction of the name, is preserved by means of a causally-based chain linking subsequent uses of that name:[5] "A speaker, using a name '*NN*' on a particular occasion will denote some item x if there is a causal chain of *reference-preserving links* leading back from his use on that occasion ultimately to the item x itself being involved in a name-acquiring transaction such as an explicit dubbing . . . "[6] Reference, in the case of a name is, therefore, a causally-based relation.

The causal theory, then, in its negative aspect, involves a critique of (i) "psychologistic" theories of reference, and (ii) description theories of names. The first of these is seen to be represented by (a) that aspect of Russell's theory which accords an epistemologically-based necessity to reference in the case of names, and (b) the Fregean thesis which makes "sense" — a mind-related notion — the determinant of reference. The second — description

---

[5] On the Kripke-Putnam version. On other versions of the causal theory, e.g., Evans', the causal relation is said to obtain between the item (the 'intended referent') and the information possessed by the speaker. See below.

[6] Evans (1973), p. 191.

theories of names – is seen to be represented by (a) Frege's thesis that sense determines reference, where "sense" is equated with descriptions which are synonymous with a name, and (b) that aspect of Russell's theory according to which ordinary proper names are held to be disguised descriptions.

The positive aspect of the causal theory however shows that, although Russell's epistemological presuppositions are dispensed with, his two-levelled semantical framework is retained. This becomes clear when we examine the notion of "indexicality" which is said to be a logical feature of names. What makes an expression indexical is its capacity to pick out some individual directly, that is, in the absence of mediation by description. Demonstratives are paradigm cases of indexicals, for demonstrative reference – e.g., "This is A" – necessitates that the individual indicated by the demonstrative be present within the sensory context of the utterance. For Russell, the directness of the relationship between an indexical expression and what it picks out is an epistemological directness. Russell's restriction of indexicality solely to the demonstratives, "I" and "this", and the relegation of ordinary proper names to the category of (disguised) descriptions is a consequence of his Cartesian belief that what is picked out by utterances of these expressions can only be something with which we are immediately and incorrigibly acquainted.

For the causal theorists, indexicality is said to be a logical feature of names. The justification for this claim is seen to lie in the fact that particular uses of a name are causally related to the event of introducing that name by means of a demonstrative.[7] In this event, the demonstrative picks out some individual by indicating (rather than by describing), and the name is conferred on what is indicated. Thus the demonstrative fixes the reference of the name in such a way that the same individual is picked out by that name on subsequent occasions of use, even though the individual may be absent from the sensory context in which the name is uttered, and even though no demonstrative indication takes

---

[7] It is not clear why *causality*, in preference to psychological considerations should be seen as a legitimate basis for something's being a genuinely *logical* feature. A discussion of the strengths and weaknesses of the causal theory is, however, beyond the scope of our present concerns, these being to show the incompatibility of that theory with Frege's own theory of sense and reference.

place when the name is used referentially on subsequent occasions. Indexicality thus need not be restricted to certain demonstatives (requiring the presence of what is indicated), but can be seen as a feature of non-demonstrative expressions which pick out the same individual in all possible worlds (i.e., rigid designators). In this way, it is claimed that the "guarantee of reference" which characterises names involves a metaphysically-based necessity, rather than an epistemologically based one.

The causal theory does allow us to distinguish semantic from personal reference, and, at the level of personal reference, admits the possibility of appealing to speaker's intentions, beliefs, etc., – what are called *epistemological* considerations – without commitment to the view that reference is determined by these considerations. For example, I may use the name, "Fred", referentially – i.e., as a name and not as an abbreviated description – and yet fail on that occasion, to pick out any individual or I may pick out the wrong individual. For the causal theorists, this possibility of failure is not a *logical* possibility for a name used referentially. It is, rather, a possibility relating to the epistemological aspects of the use of a name on a particular occasion. If the name "Fred" in "Fred is bald" fails to pick out an individual or picks out the "wrong" individual, then the sentence containing that name may be false, not because the name fails to refer, but because there is something defective in the utterer's knowledge or information about *what* individual *that* name picks out. That is to say, a particular use of a name may be an erroneous use. The speaker's belief that the name "Fred" is a name of *this* individual may be mistaken.

For the causal theorist, it is necessary to admit this kind of possibility of failure (i.e., of error) in the case of a name. For, although names are assigned to the category of indexicals (which means they are expressions for which failure of reference is a logical impossibility), they must still be distinguished from demonstratives (to avoid the Russellian consequence of a counter-intuitively restricted class of genuine names). The "epistemological" possibility of failure of reference discussed above is what distinguishes names, here. Demonstratives do not admit the possibility of error on a particular occasion of use.

But even at the level of demonstrative reference, the causal theorist can invoke the notion of a speaker's intentions[8] in indicating some object, just as he can include reference to a speaker's intentions to refer to some item on a particular occasion of use of a name.

In one sense then, the causal theory cannot be called a "non-intentional" theory of reference; The events which are linked by the reference-preserving chain can be characterised by an appeal to a speaker's (or speakers') intentions to indicate some item by means of the demonstrative, or someone's intentions to refer to the same thing that others refer to by means of the name. But this cannot be called an "intentional" theory of reference in Husserl's sense, for reference in the case of a name remains a notion set within the Russellian two-levelled framework. To see this, we might consider the theory of "personal reference" which is implied by the notion of indexicality.

The fixing of a name's reference by means of a demonstrative, e.g. "*This* is Fred", requires that
(a) there must *be* some item present within the sensory context in which the demonstrative is uttered; and,
(b) the item must be *indicated*.
Satisfaction of these joint requirements means that the indicating (in condition (b)), be construed as a "non-intentional" relation (in Husserl's sense). For, by condition (a), "X indicates some object, o", presupposes the following:

$$(\exists x)\, x = o.$$

The relation, here, is one that is unmediated by description − i.e., by the descriptive sense of the referring expression (for demonstratives have none), or by beliefs, information, etc., associated with the referring expression (for a demonstrative is not a name − it is an index; we can entertain false beliefs about *what* is indicated but the appropriate use of the index guarantees successful reference).

Indexicality − the logical feature of names − is a notion set

---

[8] The fixing of reference can be a function of the intentions of a *community* of speakers: *Cf.* Putnam's "division of linguistic labour"; see also Evans (1973).

within a two-levelled framework: Indexicals — i.e., names and demonstatives — are expressions which refer without the mediation of sense. When a notion of "sense" is incorporated into this framework, it is equated with either

> (i) descriptions which are synonymous with a name, *or*
> (ii) information, beliefs, etc., associated with a name.

On the first of these, Frege's theory of sense and reference is identified with a "description theory" of names,[9] and is criticised for failing to do justice to the way in which names actually refer. But the assumption that there *is* a distinctive way in which names refer is one that belongs to the two-levelled semantical framework, rather than to Frege's. On the second line of interpretation, sense is equated with "epistemological" aspects of the use of a name on a particular occasion. In terms of this account, sense cannot be considered *a means to* reference (in the Husserl-Frege sense), for the reference of a name is fixed, independently of any beliefs or information I may possess about the name or its bearer on a particular occasion of use. On this interpretation, "sense" *qua* the epistemological aspects of the particular use of a name is an adjunct to reference, rather than the mediator of reference.

Even if our version of the causal theory is one which accounts for "using a name to refer" in terms of speaker's (or speakers') intentions, it will still be a "non-intentional" account in Husserl's sense. Evans, for example, compares personal reference (using a name on a particular occasion to refer) with perceiving and knowing. But the latter are understood in terms of a causal, and therefore *non*-intentional relation: "Philosophers have come increasingly to realise that major concepts in epistemology and the philosophy of mind have causality embedded within them. Seeing and knowing are both good examples".[10] On this version of the causal theory, the causal relation is between "an item's states and doings and the speaker's body of information — not between the item's being dubbed with a name and the speaker's contemporary

---

[9] There are independent reasons for objecting to the identification of Fregean sense with "descriptions-synonymous-with-a-name". See Burge (1979).

[10] Evans (1973), p. 197.

use of it".[11] "Intending to refer", on this version, is a causally-based relation, rather than an intentional relation, in Husserl's sense: "We must allow then that the denotation of a name in the community will depend in a complicated way upon what those who use the term refer to, but we will so understand 'intended referent' that typically a *necessary* (but not sufficient) condition for x's being the intended referent of S's use of a name is that x should be the source of causal origin of the body of information that S has associated with the name".[12]

If personal reference, in the case of a name is, fundamentally, a causally-based relation, then it must be a non-intentional relation, in Husserl's sense. If, at the semantic level, the guarantee of reference in the case of names is explained by appeal to indexicality, then this account will also be a non-intentional account.

[11] *Ibid.*
[12] *Ibid.*, p. 198.

BIBLIOGRAPHY

This bibliography includes only works referred to in the text. Works are cited according to date of original publication. Page references are to the editions or anthologies cited below. The following abbreviations are used:

AJP: *The Australasian Journal of Philosophy*
JBSP: *The Journal of the British Society for Phenomenology*
JP: *The Journal of Philosophy*
PAS: *Proceedings of the Aristotelian Society*
PR: *Philosophical Review*
RM: *Review of Metaphysics*

Altham, J.E.J.
   (1973) "The Causal Theory of Names", *PAS* supp. vol. 47: 209–225.
Ameriks, K.
   (1977) "Husserl's Realism", *PR* 86: 498–519.
Angelelli, I.
   (1967) *Studies on Gottlob Frege and Traditional Philosophy.* Dordrecht: Reidel.
Anscombe, G.E.M.
   (1965) "The Intentionality of Sensation: A Grammatical Feature", in R.J. Butler (ed.), *Analytical Philosophy,* second series. Oxford: Blackwell, pp. 158–180.
Aquila, R.E.
   (1974) "Husserl and Frege on Meaning", *Journal of the History of Philosophy* 12: pp. 377–383.

Attig, T.
   (1980) "Husserl and Descartes on the Foundations of Philosophy", *Metaphilosophy* 11: 17–35.
Bernet, R.
   (1979) "Bedeutung und intentionales Bewusstsein. Husserl's Begriff des Bedeutungsphaenomens". *Studien zur Sprachphaenomenologie. Phaenomenologische Forschungen* Nr.8, Freiburg/München: Alber, pp. 31–64.
Brentano, F.
   (1874) *Psychology from an Empirical Standpoint (Psychologie vom empirischen Standpunkt),* translated by A.C. Rancurello, D.B. Terrell & L.L. McAlister. London: Routledge & Kegan Paul, 1973.
   (1911) "Genuine and Fictitious Objects" (from *Von der Klassification der psychischen Phänomene,* Leipzig, 1911), translated by D.B. Terrell, in Chisholm (ed.), 1960, pp. 71–75.
   (1930) *The True and the Evident (Wahrheit und Evidenz),* translated by R.M. Chisholm, I. Politzer & K.R. Fischer. London: Routledge & Kegan Paul, 1966.
Burge, T.
   (1979) "Sinning Against Frege", *PR* 88: 398–432.
Carr, D.
   (1975) "Intentionality", in E. Pivcević (ed.), (1975), pp. 17–36.
Chisholm, R.M.
   (1957) *Perceiving: A Philosophical Study.* New York: Cornell University Press.
   (1960) *(ed.) Realism and the Background of Phenomenology,* Illinois: The Free Press of Glencoe.
   (1967) "Brentano on Descriptive Psychology and the Intentional", in E.N. Lee & M. Mandelbaum (eds.), *Phenomenology and Existentialism.* Baltimore: Johns Hopkins, pp. 1–23.
Church, A.
   (1951) "The Need for Abstract Entities in Semantic Analysis". Also in J.A. Fodor & J.J. Katz (eds.), *The Structure of Language: Readings in the Philosophy of Language.* New Jersey: Prentice-Hall, 1964, pp. 437–445.

De Boer, T.
(1978) *The Development of Husserl's Thought*, translated by T. Plantinga. The Hague: Nijhoff.

Donnellan, K.S.
(1963) "Knowing What I Am Doing", *JP* 60: 401–409.
(1966) "Reference and Definite Descriptions", *PR* 75: 281–304.

Dreyfus, H.L.
(1963) "*Sinn* and Intentional Object". Also in R.C. Solomon (ed.), 1972, pp. 196–210.
(1972) "The Perpetual Noema: Gurwitsch's Crucial Contribution", in L.E. Embree (ed.), *Life-World and Consciousness*. Evanston: Northwestern University Press, pp. 135–170.
(1982) (ed.) *Husserl, Intentionality, and Cognitive Science: Recent Studies in Phenomenology*. Cambridge (Mass.): M.I.T. Press.

Dummett, M.
(1973) *Frege: Philosophy of Language*. London: Duckworth.

Evans, G.
(1973) "The Causal Theory of Names", *PAS* supp. vol. 47: 187–208.

Føllesdal, D.
(1969) "Husserl's Notion of the Noema", *JP* 66: 680–687.
(1972) "An Introduction to Phenomenology for Analytic Philosophers", in R.E. Olson & A.M. Paul (eds.), *Contemporary Philosophy in Scandinavia*. Baltimore: Johns Hopkins, pp. 417–429.

Frege, G.
(1892) "On Sense and Reference" (*Über Sinn und Bedeutung*), translated by M. Black, in P.T. Geach & M. Black (eds.), 1952, pp. 56–78.
(1893) *The Basic Laws of Arithmetic* (*Grundgesetze der Arithmetik: Begriffsschriftlich abgeleitet*), translated, edited and introduced by M. Furth. Los Angeles: University of California Press, 1964.

Frege, G.
(1894) "Review of Dr. Husserl's *Philosophie der Arithmetik*", translated by E. Kluge, *Mind* 81 (1972): 321–337.

190

(1918) "Thoughts" (*Der Gedanke*), translated by P.T. Geach & R.H. Stoothoff, in G. Frege (1977), pp. 1–30.

(1918a) "Negation" (*Die Verneinung*), translated by P.T. Geach & R.H. Stoothoff, in G. Frege (1977), pp. 31–53.

(1977) *Logical Investigations*, ed. P.T. Geach. Oxford: Blackwell, 1977.

Furth, M.

(1964) "Introduction" to the English translation of Frege (1893).

Geach, P.T.

(1972) *Logic Matters*. London: Blackwell.

Geach, P.T. & Black, M. (eds.)

(1952) *Translations from the Philosophical Writings of Gottlob Frege*. Oxford: Blackwell.

Godfrey-Smith, W.

(1979) "Thoughts of Objects", *Monist* 62: 223–237.

Harney, M.

(1983) "Review of D.W. Smith and R. McIntyre, *Husserl and Intentionality*", *AJP* 63.

Hintikka, J.

(1976) "Possible-Worlds Semantics as a Framework for Comparative and Critical Philosophy", in G. Ryle (ed.), *Contemporary Aspects of Philosophy*. Oriel Press, pp. 57–69.

Howarth, J.M.

(1980) "Franz Brentano and Object-Directedness", *JBSP* 11: 239–254.

Husserl, E.

(1891) *Philosophie der Arithmetik*. Husserliana edition, edited by L. Eley. The Hague: Nijhoff, 1970.

(1900–01) *Logical Investigations*, Volumes I & II, (*Logische Untersuchungen*), translated from the second German edition (1913) by J.N. Findlay. London: Routledge & Kegan Paul, 1970.

(1911) "Philosophy as Rigorous Science" (*Philosophie als strenge Wissenschaft*), translated by Q. Lauer, in E. Husserl, *Phenomenology and the Crisis of Philosophy*. New York: Harper & Row, 1965, pp. 71–147.

(1913) *Ideas* (*Ideen zu einer reinen Phänomenologie und phanomenologischen Philosophie*), translated by W.R. Boyce-Gibson, London: Allen & Unwin, 1969.

Kenny, A.J.P.

(1963) *Actions, Emotions and Will*. London: Routledge & Kegan Paul.

(1968) "Cartesian Privacy", in G. Pitcher (ed.), *Wittgenstein: The Philosophical Investigations*.

Kneale, W.

(1968) "Intentionality and Intensionality", *PAS* supp. vol. 42: 73–90.

Kripke, S.

(1972) "Naming and Necessity", in D. Davidson & G. Harman (eds.), *Semantics of Natural Language*. Dordrecht: Reidel, pp. 253–355.

Küng, G.

(1972) "The World as Noema and as Referent", *JBSP* 3: 15–26.

(1973) "Husserl on Pictures and Intentional Objects", *RM* 26: 670–80.

(1975) "The Phenomenological Reduction as Epoche and as Explication", *Monist* 59: 63–80.

McIntyre, R.

(1978) "Intending and Referring; A Response to Frederick Olafson". Unpublished Research Paper, Case Western Reserve University.

(1982) "Husserl's Phenomenological Conception of Intentionality and Its Difficulties", *Philosophia* 11.

McIntyre R, & Smith, D.W.

(1971) "Intentionality via Intensions", *JP* 68: 541–61.

(1965) "Husserl's Identification of Meaning and Noema", *Monist* 59: 115–132.

Mill, J.S.

(1843) *System of Logic*. London: Longman's Green & Co., New Impression, 1947.

Mohanty, J.N.

(1964) *Edmund Husserl's Theory of Meaning*. The Hague: Nijhoff.

(1974) "Husserl and Frege: A New Look at Their Relationship", *Research in Phenomenology,* 4: 51–62.

192

(1977) (ed.) *Readings on Edmund Husserl's 'Logical Investigations'.* The Hague: Nijhoff.

(1982) *Husserl and Frege.* Bloomington: Indiana University Press.

Olafson, F.

(1975) "Husserl's Theory of Intentionality in Contemporary Perspective", *Nous* 9: 73–83.

Pears, D.

(1967) *Bertrand Russell and the British Tradition in Philosophy.* London: Collins (The Fontana Library).

Pitcher, G. (ed.)

(1968) *Wittgenstein: The Philosophical Investigations.* London: Macmillan.

Pivcević, E. (ed.)

(1975) *Phenomenology and Philosophical Understanding.* Cambridge: Cambridge University Press.

Prior, A.N.

(1968) "Intentionality and Intensionality", *PAS* supp. vol. 42: 91–106.

(1971) *Objects and Thought* (ed. P.T. Geach & A.J.P. Kenny). Oxford: Oxford University Press.

Putman, H.

(1975) "The Meaning of 'Meaning'", in H. Putnam, *Mind, Language and Reality: Philosophical Papers.* Cambridge: Cambridge University Press, §12.

Quine, W.V.O.

(1948) "On What There Is", in W.V.O. Quine (1953), §1, pp. 1–19.

(1950) "Identity, Ostension and Hypostasis", in W.V.O. Quine (1953), §IV, pp. 65–79.

(1953) *From a Logical Point of View.* New York: Harper & Row, (1953), second, revised edition, 1961.

(1953a) "On Mental Entities", in W.V.O. Quine (1966), §18, pp. 208–214.

(1956) "Quantifiers and Propositional Attitudes", in W.V.O. Quine (1966), §15, pp. 183–194.

(1960) *Word and Object.* Massachusetts: Massachusetts Institute of Technology Press.

(1966) *The Ways of Paradox and Other Essays.* New York: Random House.

(1968) "Ontological Relativity" in W.V.O. Quine, *Ontological Relativity and Other Essays,* New York: Columbia University Press, 1969, §2.

(1973) *The Roots of Reference.* The Paul Carus Lectures. Illinois: Open Court.

Quinton, A.M.

(1964) "Contemporary British Philosophy". Excerpt in G. Pitcher (ed.), 1968, pp. 1–21.

Russell, B.

(1903) *The Principles of Mathematics.* London: Allen & Unwin, 1956. (seventh impression).

(1904) "Meinong's Theory of Complexes and Assumptions", in B. Russell (1973), pp. 21–76.

(1905) "On Denoting", in B. Russell (1973), pp. 103–119.

(1912) *The Problems of Philosophy.* London: Oxford University Press, 1962.

(1914) "On the Nature of Acquaintance", in B. Russell (1956), pp. 125–174.

(1918) "The Philosophy of Logical Atomism", in B. Russell (1956), pp. 175–281.

(1921) *The Analysis of Mind.* London: Allen & Unwin, 1961 (eighth impression).

(1940) *An Inquiry into Meaning and Truth.* London: Allen & Unwin, 1943 (second impression).

(1956) *Logic and Knowledge* (ed. R.C. Marsh). London: Allen & Unwin, 1956.

(1973) *Essays in Analysis* (ed. D. Lackey). New York: George Braziller, 1973.

Russell, B. & Whitehead, A.N.

(1913) *Principia Mathematica.* Cambridge: Cambridge University Press, 1962.

Ryle, G.

(1949) *The Concept of Mind.* Middlesex: Penguin, 1966.

Searle, J.R.

(1958) "Russell's Objections to Frege's Theory of Sense and Reference", *Analysis* 18: 137–143.

Smith, B.

(1978) "Frege and Husserl: The Ontology of Reference", *JBSP* 9: 111–125.

194

Smith, D.W.
   (1982) "Husserl on Demonstrative Reference and Perception",
        in H.L. Dreyfus (ed.).
Smith, D.W. & McIntyre, R.
   (1982) *Husserl and Intentionality. A Study of Mind, Meaning
        and Language.* Dordrecht: Reidel.
Solomon, R.C.
   (1970) "Sense and Essence: Frege and Husserl", in R.C.
        Solomon (ed.), 1972, pp. 258–282.
   (1972) (ed.) *Phenomenology and Existentialism.* New York:
        Harper & Row.
Thiel, C.H.
   (1968) *Sense and Reference in Frege's Logic.* Dordrecht: Reidel.
Willard, D.
   (1980) "Husserl on a Logic That Failed", *PR* 89: 46–64.

INDEX